EXTRAORDINARY PARTIES

Your step-by-step guide to planning luxury creative events, celebrations, weddings and dinner parties.

DEBBIE MARKS

CONTENTS

"FIND YOUR SPARKLE,

|

DISCOVER
WHAT'S POSSIBLE,

|

LIVE
EXTRAORDINARY."

|

DEBBIE MARKS

LIVE YOUR EXTRAORDINARY

Chapter One

INTRODUCTION

*H*ello! I'm so excited that you've got this book in your hands right now! Perhaps you're going to be planning (or considering planning) a special celebration at some point soon. Maybe you're just looking for some creative inspiration to make your next events even more exciting and magical!

Whatever the occasion, however intimate or grand, planning a unique and memorable event can seem daunting. I understand how much you desperately want to create something extraordinary! You already know the basics of what you want: an amazing look, for your guests to have the best time ever, and to create the most wonderful memory for your friends and family (the kind they'll talk about for years to come) - but... you *don't* know **how to pull it all together.** Take a deep breath, there's no need to panic because I've got you. Relax and enjoy the journey I'm about to take you on.

If you could wave a magic wand right now and bring your dream event to life, what would it look like?

You might have hundreds of ideas in your head, but no idea where to start. That's okay. You may feel overwhelmed by the thought of it all because you want to host an event you can look back at and think *"that was one of the best experiences of my life!"* This book is going to help YOU become the perfect host!

Shhh. . . this is just between us. I'm all about making you *look good*, so your secret's safe with me.

I'm here to hold your hand every step of the way to ensure your celebration is truly magical. My goals are to make your event planning a breeze *and* to help you enjoy each part of the process. If you're a professional (or aspiring) event planner, then this book will become your events bible! Keep it on your desk - anytime you want some inspiration or creative ideas, you can pop in and out of here as needed.

I'd highly recommend reading this book from cover to cover. There are some hidden gems you won't want to miss! This is the kind of guide you're going to want to keep somewhere safe, so you can open it up for inspo whilst planning special occasions over the years. You'll find tips for planning weddings, parties, entertaining at home, bar/bat mitzvahs, special birthdays, lifecycle events, and seasonal celebrations such as summer parties or creating an epic Christmas at home. If you're planning as you read, pop onto my website to download my free 'Celebration Planner Workbook' for making notes as you go.

Let me officially introduce myself, since we're going to be spending some quality time together. I always say to my event planning clients, you've got to feel super comfortable and chilled with the person who's helping you plan such an important moment. So, hello! I'm Debbie Marks, a luxury event designer and stylist based in Manchester, UK.

When it comes to planning epic events, you're in good hands! I've been planning and designing luxury events for over 23 years.

There are more than 1,500 events under my belt - in various shapes and sizes - that I have been part of all over the world. I've got an overactive creative brain and a passion for celebrating. Prepare yourself to be buzzing with ideas by the time you get to the end of this book.

I'm known for planning elaborate creative weddings, private parties, and bar/bat mitzvahs. I have a first-class BA (Hons) in Event Management, so for pretty much my entire life, I have been living and breathing events! I'm also the official stylist for the Queen Charlotte's Ball, the flagship event for the London Season and other royal events. From lavish parties in back garden marquees to intimate dinner parties and celebrations in private residences, I love planning memorable occasions. I've had the honour of putting together creative gala dinners for some of the world's largest brands, as well as parties for celebrities and foot-ballers. It's definitely in my blood, but I've got it down to an art form.

The most common things my clients say to me are, "You look so chilled," and "You were so calm and super easy to deal with." Well yes, that's me in a nutshell. I'm a really hard worker. I get incredibly passionate about your event! There's nothing quite like that moment when I'm with clients and the penny drops as I know I've nailed how to pull their vision together in my head. I'm usually jumping up and down, buzzing with excitement because I can see it all coming together and how fabulous it's going to look. Many of my clients who have worked with me on more than one occasion have just learnt to trust me now - they know it's going to be epic!

I can't wait to get started! I'm ready to spill the beans and share *all* my expert event planning tips so you can make **your special occasion** one to remember. This book is designed to make your event planning easy. You'll be able to take my tips and implement them for your own events. Whether you're planning a baby shower, dinner party, a wedding, or a larger party, the principles I'll be sharing with you remain the same. You can use these *'secrets'* to make your special occasions **extraordinary** and let's be honest here... *life's too short for boring parties.*

My aim is to leave you feeling like *you've got this,* inspire you to make your events more creative, and help you feel confident in the exact steps you'll take to plan and implement the perfect party. I'm a strong believer that we *all* should take the opportunity to **celebrate every moment possible:** every birthday, valentine's, graduation, baby shower, and more! What's life for if we can't share these special moments with friends and family?

For the purpose of this book, I'm going to use the word 'Party' a lot when it comes to referring to your event. PARTY. The dictionary describes the meaning of PARTY as "A social gathering of invatationd guests, typically involving eating, drinking and entertainment" But if it's ok with you, I'm going to add to this... fabulous decor & magic touches that create the most incredible memories for your guests!

Every year, as I'm designing over 300 events, so many clients bring me their Pinterest boards. They tell me they've pinned lots of their favourites, but have no idea how any of them work together. This is where I come into my element! I've made sense of hundreds of confused couples' wedding and event decor. It's delightful to watch people transform from being overwhelmed at the start to complete joy when they see everything come to life.

Throughout this book I'm going to take you on a journey, showing you exactly what steps you need to take to plan an extraordinary event! We'll cover where to start and how to bring your event to life:

- create a vision for your event
- generate a buzz from the outset
- design a luxury table

- dress your home or venue
- make food and drink exciting
- bring entertainment into your event
- make milestone events special (such as birthdays, baby showers, bridal showers, bar/bat mitzvahs, and anniversaries)
- create extraordinary seasonal celebrations in your home all year round
- make all of this stress-free (which for me, is the most important part).

I want you to enjoy this entire process, let me tell you some more...

PS: If you're a budding event planner reading this, or if this is a career you're hoping to get into, guard this book with your life and take it everywhere you go. I promise you; it will help you with the planning of your events for years to come!

"TO CREATE SOMETHING EXCEPTIONAL, YOUR MINDSET MUST BE RELENTLESSLY ON THE SMALLEST OF DETAILS"

INSPIRED BY GIORGIO ARMANI

Chapter Two

GETTING INTO THE ZONE

S o, here's the thing, I'm a true entrepreneur at heart. I've worked my arse off for years growing my events business and have enjoyed every moment... BUT for me, it's never been all about the money. It's more than just work. Creating gorgeous memories for my clients is a labour of love.

The problem was, I hadn't been showing that same level of love and care to myself. Something had to change. I'm still on this journey, but now I appreciate the importance of making an effort to spend quality time with friends and family. I want to make those moments special - for myself and for them.

This is my mission now: to enjoy life to the fullest, to create beautiful memories for myself and my family whilst *helping you do the same*. Life is too short! You blink and your kids have grown up. Make the most of each special occasion as these are the memories that we keep with us forever.

Abundance comes to me in the form of happiness, the memories I create, and the special events I celebrate with my friends and family. *This* is what makes me successful. I can't wait for all the joyful moments that are about to happen! Nothing delights me more than creating unique and memorable celebrations for my clients, friends, and family.

When my mum visits me from London, we go for long walks together through the countryside here in Manchester. As we walk, I tell her stories of the latest events I've designed and styled, the fabulous entertainment, and all the details. I talk about decor a lot, making things look pretty, transforming boring rooms into spectacular spaces, or making a table look fabulous. These things excite me and I love coming up with crazy ideas wherever I go - taking inspiration from my travels, shopping experiences, restaurants, or architecture. My eyes are always wandering, my mind goes into creative overdrive, and ideas start formulating in my head!

My mum once asked me, "What is it that makes you love what you do so much? Why is it that you love encouraging people to make things look nice?" Yes, I might get to play with beautiful decor all day long, but the live events industry is one I'm incredibly passionate about. It's often an industry that gets ignored, one that's full of talented, hard-working people. This is how I described it to my mum . . .

*When you go walking in the woods - with all the beautiful trees and greenery around you, the sunlight shining through the trees, the birds singing, and the dewdrops glistening - how does it make you feel? For me, it's a feeling of calm, relaxation, and tranquility. If you were to go for the same walk along a busy road with lots of cars and pollution, would you **feel** the **same** way?* Her answer was no and I'd bet you agree with her. I went on to explain that **how we decorate our surroundings has a huge impact** on feelings, changing our state, and our overall experience.

The exact same principle applies to our events, however big or small. **The way we transform a space makes a difference.** Sitting down at a plain table is *not the same* as having a beautifully dressed table laden with decor, stylish plates, cutlery, glassware, and fabulous centrepieces, in a room that's been fully kitted out with draping, suspended floral installations and atmospheric lighting. It creates an **experience**. It gives your guests the WOW factor.

Decor also gets people talking. I'm currently writing this book from a sun lounger overlooking an infinity pool in a beautiful villa in Ibiza. I'm supremely grateful to be here in these exquisite surroundings. Last night we made a BBQ. My friend David, who loves to cook, provided the food and I decorated the table. Everyone was so surprised and happy at the effort I put in to make the dining experience extra special for them.

Have you ever cooked a meal for your guests and family that they've really enjoyed? Odds are, your satisfaction from their happy reaction far outweighed the effort you had put in. The same truth applies to decor. It's amazing to see others having a great time at your events! You'll often see me at the back of a wedding just enjoying the special feeling of watching people celebrate in a space and environment I created.

We're a generation now that wants to be entertained, that wants more than the everyday norm. We want to be surprised, we want to be made to feel special, we want to *experience the extraordinary*! This is exactly what I'm going to show you how to do in this book. **It's your surroundings that make the difference.**

As the host, you have the opportunity to create a magical experience for your guests. Food plays a role and you may revel in feeding your guests delicious dishes until they want to burst! But you also want them to walk away with beautiful memories of their time with you. I'm going to show you how to take entertaining to the *next level* so you can realise the possibilities. You'll **learn how easy it can be** to take a special occasion and transform it into something **exceptional** that your *guests will love*, one you'll all be talking about for years to come.

I'm a strong believer that life is for living - so seize every chance you can to make it as special as possible. You could dress your home to reflect the joys of each season or celebrate each birthday and life cycle event in its own unique way. From the moment they walk through the door, your guests will appreciate the festive and memorable atmosphere, along with the effort you've made to create it.

As you read this book the first time, you might feel lost on where to start. Just the thought of entertaining can seem daunting. I totally get it and I'm here to be the secret sauce to your next event (shhh! I won't tell) and help *you* shine as the hostess with the mostest!

This book will take the pressure off. Inside its pages you'll find loads of creative new ideas to excite, entertain, and wow your guests. Imagine yourself as the hostess of **extraordinary events** that show people you care and you've made an effort (but without the hassle you might expect).

Next time you have an occasion to treat yourself for achieving something special, you might find an event is a better alternative than buying designer shoes or handbags. With your creativity unleashed, you'll be able to confidently plan celebrations that suit your budget and your vision. I'm here to help you take the stress out of the planning so that you can get started right away.

The process of entertaining can be magical, enjoyable, and rewarding! As you read through this book, relax and let your mind explore the possibilities.

Are you ready? Let's do this . . .

"WE DON'T REMEMBER THE DAYS, BUT RATHER THE MOMENTS"

Chapter Three

CREATING YOUR VISION

I'm so excited! Let's get started. We're going to bring your vision to life! In this chapter, we're going to start planning your event. By the end of it, you'll be in a really good place, knowing exactly how to move forward. You might be reading this book for leisure right now **or** you can actually use this book to *implement* as we go. Within the chapters, you'll find handy checklists along the way. Remember you can also download my "*Celebration Planner workbook*" at www.debbie-marks.com.

We're putting you in the hot seat right now as you determine all the details of your next event. I'm a big fan of making event planning easy, so I'm going to talk you through the questions you need to be asking yourself. My first suggestion: write down all your answers so you get a really good picture of what you're doing (hint, you can download your celebration planner to organise your notes). If you're planning far ahead for a dream event, you can use this book to create your *event vision board*. Then, frame it and put it in a prime position where you'll see it every day. This will allow amazing things to come to you because your best vision of the event will remain in the back of your mind.

As we go, I'll share with you examples from a very personal event I'm planning (whilst writing my first book, of course). By the time you read this, the big day will have happened. In February 2022, I'm hosting a Batmitzvah party for my oldest daughter, Dahlia. In case you're unfamiliar with the term Batmitzvah, I'll briefly explain it here. It's a coming-of-age party that follows a religious ceremony for a Jewish boy (a Barmitzvah) or girl (a Batmitzvah) to commemorate that they are officially obligated to follow the Jewish laws.

These celebrations are always full of life and laughter! The parties are incredible and I love them for their creativity. Every Bat/Bar-mitzvah reception is different, quirky, and full of special touches that make it wonderfully meaningful for friends and family. It's a true milestone in a Jewish child's life. I started planning these events over 13 years ago and this is where I truly found my calling and creative outlet.

Whatever the occasion, there are a few key things you need to know as you begin planning your event. To get you started thinking, let's dive into my questions for you.

1) Who is the event for? This is an easy question to determine the nature of the event. This also might become the name of your event.

In my case, it's Dahlia's Batmitzvah. I've decided to call my event Dahlia-Fest. You'll find out why shortly.

2) How many guests would you like to invatation? Obviously, this is an important factor in determining your costs as well as the size of your venue. I'll tell you later how to make the planning of your guest list super easy.

We're planning on having 120 guests. The way we worked this out was I made a list of family we wanted to invatation, then a list of our friends and I asked Dahlia to make a list of the friends she wanted to invatation.

3) What's the format of your event? What do you want to happen at your event? For example, will it be a formal lunch, afternoon tea, a garden party, or an evening party? It's helpful here to determine what food and drink you want to offer as this will determine a lot of the structure of your event.

What kind of vibe do you want to create? It could be informal, formal, fun, family-friendly, or an adults-only party. Do you want your event to be full of surprises? How long do you want your event to last? The planning of a big event is all part of the fun so allow yourself to enjoy the process.

This was easy for me as I've been dreaming of planning this particular event for years! However, I did have to talk it through with my husband and daughter as their input was also really important to me.

We decided we wanted to have fun with our event. We wanted lots of interactive elements and of course we wanted to blow our guests away with the decor and special little touches. One important aspect for us was to mark the religious element of this event. After all, this will be a big life moment for Dahlia, so we are going to have a small ceremony at the beginning of our evening before we go into one mega party. We also wanted to incorporate a sit-down meal and lots of dancing!

4) Where would you like to host your event? Take time now to determine your venue? What space do you have to work with? What is important to you in terms of location?

You may know the answer to this question (i.e., if you're having the event at home), but please consider what space you have and how many guests you can comfortably accommodate.

For events outside your home, make sure you take into account the following when choosing your venue:

- Proximity to the majority of your guests - how far will they need to travel to get there?
- Event budget - venues vary drastically in prices: anything

from a few £100's for a village hall to £1000's for a top London hotel.

- How does the venue reflect the vibe you want to create?
- For example, rustic (a barn) or urban (a warehouse), modern, luxury, historic, etc...
- Do you want the venue to be an experience (i.e., in a castle or a museum)?
- Do you have space for a marquee in your back garden?
- Does the space have an area for a cocktail reception (if you're planning on having one)?
- Will the bar be in the same room?
- What are the toilets like? Are there enough, accessibility, condition?

I've created you a checklist of things to look out for/questions to ask at your venue when planning an event.

If you're planning an event at home, you'll find dedicated sections on this later in the book. If you are considering using your home as your event space, the two most important questions to ask yourself are:

1. How many guests are you planning on inviting? and
2. Do you have the space to host your event? Either inside or outside?

There is something incredibly special about hosting an event in your own home and welcoming your guests into your living space.

We chose to have Dahlia's Batmitzvah at the Victoria & Albert Marriott in Manchester. The main reasons for our venue choice: location (it's easy for our guests to travel there) and size (the space is the perfectly suited for our guest numbers, not too big or too small).

For our event, the space will act as a completely blank canvas. It doesn't really matter what the carpet and walls look like now. I'm going to completely trans-

form the space to create a beautiful experience for our guests. The hotel foyer has also recently been refurbished so the luxury vibe begins on arrival. I advise going for site visits when looking for the perfect venue. Remember to ask if they have any planned renovation works, too.

Another factor for me was being familiar with the venue. I've been styling events there for years. It's a special place as I know how many amazing memories I've created there. The hotel staff are super friendly, too.

5) What would you like the theme of your event to be?

Creating a theme for your event makes it truly unique and extraordinary. A theme adds fun and impact. It provides a structure for you to wow your guests and create incredible memories.

I like to think every event needs a theme. It doesn't need to be a full-on theme (however, these are really fun). Maybe it's a colour scheme, or themed around a name like Rose, a particular occasion, season, or favourite movie. A theme is where the magic comes in: you can tie it to the whole experience, from the invitations right through to every detail on the big day, including the entertainment. I'm going to talk you through all these steps later on in the book, but let's start with deciding on the theme you're going to choose.

First, think of the guest of honour. Consider their personality, favourite holiday destination, movie, sports team, colour or colour combination. Perhaps they have a favourite nightclub or a restaurant.

Recently, I've planned events for a client who's a huge fan of a cabaret restaurant called Lio's in Ibiza. Deborah was meant to celebrate her 40th birthday there. It got cancelled due to the Covid pandemic. Instead, we recreated a Lio's themed party in her own home, packed with entertainment, showgirls, sequins, dramatic food and drinks. This particular client had a pool in the basement of her house, so we covered over the pool and turned it into a dancefloor. I'll explain more about this party as we go.

There are hundreds of themes you could choose from. On page 31, you'll find a list with some of my favourites for inspiration. You can use these for a small intimate dinner party, a garden party, or a full-on themed event. I've categorised them for you to help make choosing your theme easier.

The theme for Dahlia's batmitzvah is 'DahliaFest'. We chose this fun concept to celebrate how she puts her own stamp on things. Dahlia loves the festival vibe! Her bedroom features ethereal colours and a dream catcher. Dahlia is very creative and loves to do things in her own way. That spirit will shine through in every aspect of her party.

6) How would you like to serve food at your event?

The time of day has a big impact on other elements of your event, such as the seating and room layout arrangements.

This question is more about **how** you would like to *serve food*, rather than what style of food you will choose, which will come later.

Here's a few suggestions for you based on the time of day for your event. We'll go into food & drink a lot more later on in the book.

Morning Event
Breakfast
Brunch Buffet
Bottomless Brunch

Lunch
Seated Served Lunch
Buffet Lunch
Food Stations

Afternoon
Afternoon Tea
Buffet

Evening
Standing Reception
Seated Served Dinner
Buffet
Food Stations

Think about if you want your guests to eat standing or seated. Do you want them at formal dining tables or would you like more of a chilled-out vibe, with tall poseur tables and stools and casual seating? Knowing this will really help with planning out the style of food you choose.

For Dahlia's Batmitzvah, it will be a drinks reception with lots of substantial quirky canapés, a Sushi and Miso station and a Barbacoa and Guacamole bar with pulled lamb and beef chuck. We are then serving a sit-down dinner. We're not doing a starter, but will be serving food family-style with a mini buffet in the centre of each of the guests' banqueting tables - I want them to be overflowing with food. For dessert, we're going to do an incredible edible garden dessert buffet. It's going to be a bit of a feature! I'm definitely a feeder, and want there to be plenty of food for everyone.

7) Determine your budget for your event

This is a really important topic and often one that might put people off for planning events. In life, we need to prioritize how we spend our money. I'd rather spend it on things that will create amazing memories for me and my family, but also for others too and that's really special.

When setting your budget, be as flexible as possible. Budget might not be an issue and you're happy to spend whatever it takes to create the event you desire. Set yourself an "In an ideal world" budget but also an "if I want to make it extra special, I could stretch to…" budget.

It's easy to spend money when it comes to events, so be prepared for all the gorgeous extras that add the special touches and magic details. I always say whatever your budget is, if you spend it in the right way, on the things that are going to make the most impact, you can't go wrong. I always find that some people have different priorities when it comes to events, some want fabulous food, others the best entertainment, for some it's all about location, or mind-blowing decor... many of my clients want it all! Think about your priorities, what's the most important thing for you?

I often get asked, how much do I need to spend on an event. This is a really hard question to answer, it's like asking me how much do I need to buy a car? Do you want a Ford Fiesta or a Lamborghini? The more you spend, the better quality and experience you get, it's as simple as that.

But, please note, there is nothing wrong with a Ford Fiesta. If you're on a lemonade budget with champagne taste, don't let that limit your creativity. The most incredible memories can happen on a budget.

When I was growing up, I was heavily involved with youth work and creating informal educational activities for kids. I remember transforming bland sports halls into full-on cultural marketplaces - all on a shoestring of a budget. We *had* to think out of the box and come up with unique, creative ideas to make these events happen. The end result was always memorable and incredible! Often, creating the event was as fun as delivering the event itself. The big question to ask yourself is what are your top 'Must Haves?'

Dahlia's Batmitzvah - I've agreed on a budget with my husband. I'm used to dealing with affluent clients with event budgets of £100,000+. My budget is nowhere near this, so I am going to be creative, thinking where I want to make the impact, and work from there.

8) Determine your Why?

This is the mushy part for me. I dig deep into my heart and look at why I'm putting this event on. Is it because you want to spoil someone special? Do you want to treat yourself and celebrate your business successes with friends and family? Has your son or daughter worked particularly hard and you want to give them an extra-fun and memorable birthday this year?

Know your why and think what the most incredible party would mean to you. Now close your eyes and start visualising what this could look like.

How do you feel? How are your guests feeling? Are there certain things like entertainment or food or activities that are coming prominent in your visions?

Write all these things down as these will be the most important elements you want to bring into your event. When it comes to planning, these are the key things you'll focus on to make sure it's exceptionally special.

My why for Dahlia's Batmitzvah is so much more than honoring a milestone moment in her life. Yes, this moment is important and it's the official reason we're doing a special event. It was meant to take place last year; however, the pandemic didn't allow us to host a big party. As I create extraordinary parties for a living, I couldn't let this moment pass without doing something especially meaningful for Dahlia and our friends and family.

In some ways, this is my little reward for working hard throughout the years. Even more than that, I want my family to experience the pure joy of organising a special event! Since Dahlia was a little girl, she's been talking about what she wants her party to look like. I remember when she was younger, she always used to tell me she wanted a red carpet and a shiny glitter ball (we've come a lot further than this now, but will always remember these discussions).

Now you've got the outline of your event. You know the key moving parts or you've started to visualise what your event is going to look like. The next step of this journey is to show you how to create an extraordinary event. This is when the fun begins!

9) Choose your date.

Once you have determined your whys, let's take the first step to making it happen and fix a date!

Checklist: Questions to ask yourself at the beginning of your planning process.

1) Who's your event for? _____

2) How many guests? _____

3) What's the format of your event?_____

4) Where are you going to host your event?_____

5) What theme would you like for your event?

_____

6) How would you like to serve food at your event?

_____

7) Determine your budget & what are your top Must Haves

_____

. . .

8) Determine your Why _____

9) Choose your date _____

―――――――

LIST OF PARTY AND EVENT THEME IDEAS

Colour Combos

Dove grey and baby pink
Emerald green, gold and white
Royal blue & yellow
Baby pink & rose gold
Pretty in Pink
Black with any of the following: silver, gold, orange, green, pink, red, purple, yellow, white
Pastels - lemon, lilac, pale pink & sage green
Hot pink & black
White
Red, Blue, Green, Yellow - Great for a pop art/Lego theme
Silver Soiree
Turquoise and hot pink
Neons/Glow in the dark
Paint the town red

Movie/TV/Book inspired themes

Alice In Wonderland/Mad hatters tea party
Star Wars
Great Gatsby
James Bond
Moulin Rouge
Dirty Dancing

Greece
Bridgerton
The Chronicles of Narnia
The Little Mermaid
Pirates of the Caribbean
Sex & the City
The Devil Wears Prada
Mean Girls
Dumbo
Greatest Showman
Friends
Harry Potter
Charlie & the Chocolate Factory
Wizard of Oz
Beauty & the Beast
Mary Poppins
Night at the Museum
Frozen
Superheroes
Mama Mia
The Godfather
Casino Royale
Disney

Nature inspired themes

Enchanted
Winter Wonderland
Tropical
Flamingo Luau
Under the Sea
Neon Jungle
Tropical Jungle
English Country Garden
Festival Glam

Boho Chic

World themes

Futuristic/Space
Ancient Egyptian
Caribbean
Hollywood
Italian Garden
Quintessentially British
Vegan
Tribal
Wild West
Japan
Rio
Parisian Party
Greek Night
Moroccan
Arabian Nights
Burlesque
Hawaiian Luau
American

Spring Themes

In bloom
Cherry blossom
Lemon and limes
Valentines
Mothers Day
Easter
Woodland

Summer Themes

Club Tropicana
Carnival
Festival - Coachella Style!
African
Boho Vibes
Pretty in Pink
Moroccan Nights
Mediterranean
White Party
Champagne & Caviar
Mardi Gras
Midsummer Night's Dream
Footloose
Glamping
Bohemian Nights

Autumn

Circus Freak show
Halloween
Haunted House
Autumn
Oktoberfest
Fall into Autumn

Winter

Winter Wonderland
Bavarian
Après Ski
Rustic Christmas
Traditional Christmas
Aspen Forest

Champagne Luxe
Winter Frost

Era Inspired Themes

Roaring 20s
Vintage
60s Summer of Love
70s
Retro Disco
Wartime
Victorian
Masked Ball
Speakeasy
Hoedown
Disco Inferno
Medieval Banquet
Dinosaurs

Other

Urban Graffiti
Fire & Ice
Diamonds are Forever
Unicorn
Fairytale
Bubbles & Bowties
Denim & Diamonds

LIST OF QUESTIONS TO ASK AT POTENTIAL VENUES

What are the capacities of the room? i.e., how many people can the room hold.

You will need to know what layout you want, e.g., seated at round tables, casual seating & standing reception etc.

Ask for a floor plan/dimensions of the room. This will come in really handy when you get to the styling stages.

How much does it cost to hire the space? Here's some specific questions to ask around cost:

How long do you get the space for within this rate?

What's the earliest your suppliers can get access to set up the room?

Do suppliers need to depart the room by a certain time?

What's included within the price?

Does it include food/drink and if so, what are your options?

Will you be able to discuss menus with the chef?

If you are dry hiring the space (e.g., bringing in your own caterer), note not all venues allow this, so ask the question if it's part of your plans. You might do this if you would like a specific type of catering (e.g., Kosher, Halal, Caribbean, etc.) If you are going down this route, ask the venue if you can also bring in your own bar and whether they charge corkage for doing this.

Check out the toilets

I find you can tell a lot about a venue from how their toilets look, so when I go into a venue I always pop in for a quick, intentional 'toilet stop'. You might have a gorgeous ballroom, but if the toilets look like a school locker room, it certainly won't help to create a luxury feel.

If you're in love with the main space, but the toilets are lacking, you could always spruce them up for your event. Put in an arrangement of fresh flowers, add a perfume diffuser, some luxury soaps, and hand wash for a quick upgrade. Top it all off with a vanity basket, full of amenities for your guests.

- Access for suppliers - how easy is it for your suppliers to get into your venue. If you know you need specific things and your venue is on the top floor, how big is the lift, will everything fit? The more information you can provide for your suppliers, the more they will love you! There is nothing worse than getting to a venue to find out your dancefloor won't fit in the lift! (Trust me, my team have experienced it!)
- Will they allow you to use haze? You only need to ask this question if you are planning on having lots of feature lighting in the room. Haze allows the beams of light to become visible, making lighting come to life. It also diffuses the light meaning it's less harsh to look directly into. If they do allow haze you will need to get the venue to isolate the fire alarms in the room. If they allow it, they will be used to doing this.
- Can you fit the layout you want in the room? You can ask the venue to create a floor plan for you.
- Is there a bar in the room? I always prefer it when the bar is inside the room as it always keeps your guests with the main space which stops you from losing atmosphere. Also, if you are using theatrics at your bar, I always like it when guests can see this too.
- How much power does the venue have? If you are bringing in lots of equipment that requires power, please ask this question. You might need to check with your suppliers how much power they require and then ask the venue. The last thing you want is fuses blowing on the night and all the music and everything switching off.

- Is the venue hosting any open days? It's always nice to go view the venue where they have it set up for an event. Sometimes venues will allow you to see the space set up for another event just before it starts, so make sure you ask the question.
- Do they allow real flame? As a decor specialist and a lover of candlelight, this question is really important.
- Who will you be working with from the venue? I always think it's important to work with a venue that is willing to meet your requirements. Building a relationship with your key contact at the venue is really important to ensure you get everything you have asked for on the day.

VANITY/PAMPER EVENT BASKET CHECKLIST

I always love to include the following in my baskets. You can do this for events at home or at outside venues. It's a really nice touch that guests appreciate.

- Deodorant
- Perfume/Body Spray
- Hair Spray
- Band-Aids/Plasters, Blister plasters, Party Feet
- Hand sanitiser
- Tissues
- Dry Shampoo
- Wet Wipes/Face Wipes
- Feminine Hygiene Products
- Hair Brush
- Hair Grips/Bobby Pins
- Clear Nail varnish
- Lash Glue
- Vaseline
- Toothpicks
- Safety Pins

- Sewing Kit
- Hair Gel
- Double sided (boob) tape
- Natural Tights
- Mints
- Sunscreen (for outdoor weddings in hot settings)
- Bug spray (for outdoor weddings in hot settings)
- Lollipops

For a welcoming touch, add a cute little sign with a message like;

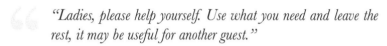

"Ladies, please help yourself. Use what you need and leave the rest, it may be useful for another guest."

— *COMPLIMENTS OF THE NEWLYWEDS.*

"THE DIFFERENCE
BETWEEN ORDINARY
AND
EXTRAORDINARY
IS THE EXTRA DETAILS
THE
MAGIC TOUCHES."

Chapter Four

MAKING YOUR EVENT EXTRAORDINARY

*G*et ready to unleash your creativity and let your mind run wild! The craziest ideas can transform into the fabulous touches that make your event the highlight of the year. These elements are often referred to as "creative, quirky, or *magic* touches." They are the things that make your guests say *Ooh! What a fabulous idea!*

You'll find loads of ideas in this book that are suitable for any style of event, from a wedding to a kid's party and more. Think of these as suggestions to get you excited. Then make it yours by putting your own unique twist on things.

As I was writing the last chapter, my creative brain went into overdrive, imagining the most epic parties with all the different themes. One day, most (maybe all) of these larger-than-life parties will become a reality - if I've not created them yet. Certainly, they'll be filled with an abundance of the creative details that make each event extraordinary.

There are 100's of ideas I could give you for this, but I'm going to share with you my top 10 'Creative Touches' that you could incorporate into your events. Next time you attend an event, you'll notice these special details even more - and you'll definitely notice if there aren't any.

Creative Touches produce the Magic . . .

1) Wave that wand from the very beginning

If you're going to create an 'Extraordinary Event' then the excitement, or 'event buzz' needs to start from the moment you send your invitations out!

The invitation will definitely set the tone of your event, so make sure it looks the part. Invitations can be electronic or through the post - both types can be equally impressive.

Some of my favourite invitations I've created over the years include a ski pass that came complete with snow in the invatation. For a car-themed bar mitzvah, the invitation was a smart acrylic invitation made to look like traffic lights. For my daughter Dahlia, I did a giant festival pass on a hot pink lanyard with foil printing. This came in a turquoise padded envelope with gold confetti inside.

For an easy way to send an online invitation, try websites such as www.paperlesspost.com or www.greenevelope.com. Or go extravagant online by creating a customised video/film to email your guests as an invatation. If money was no object, I would have a mini customised film created that turns into an invitation. Or you could double it up with a super cool invatation that has a website link on it. When your guests visit the website, your video is waiting there to share all the event details.

I love using unusual textures for event invitations. Also, remember the envelope needs to be as quirky as the invatation itself. To make your invitation look and feel more special, try padded envelopes, invatations in boxes, foiled envelopes, funky inner linings, or a lovely textured envelope. Add more style by closing your envelope with a personalised wax seal or a sticker designed to match the event theme.

If you've opted for a hard copy invatation, create something that will have your guests excited or intrigued to know more about the event activities. Use a quirky dress code, create a funky name for your event, and incorporate the event theme terminology onto your invatation. E.g., If you've chosen a football theme,

"Kick-Off: 7 pm. Full Time: 1 am."

You can adapt this concept to suit your chosen theme.

2) Brand Your Event/Create a Logo for your event

Having a logo for your event is both fun and useful. Logos open up a new world of possibilities to make each component unique and special to your event. You might think logos are only for businesses, so, let's take a moment to explore: why does a company have a logo?

A logo is used to create attraction, familiarisation, and a visual representation of who we are and what we're about. We can do exactly the same for our events. Your event represents you! Having a strong logo, colour scheme, and vibe from the start will create an identity for your event and how you want it to be perceived. A logo can determine whether your event is more sophisticated or playful and once you have a logo/concept for your event, there are so many things you can do with it!

Here's a few ideas of how you can you use your logo once you have it:

- On your invatations, of course!
- Signage
- Doormats
- Personalised napkins

- Coasters
- Cushions
- Front of your Bar, DJ Booth
- Bar/Food Menus
- Favours
- Take home bags
- Branded apparel
- Entrance signage
- Branded bags for gifts
- Printed on your dancefloor
- Light projections
- Printed on Ice Cream Wafers

Recently, I planned an extraordinary 40th birthday party - Deborah's 40th we learnt about earlier. This featured a brand concept throughout the entire event. We had a colour scheme (black, red, silver & gold) for all of the event decor, and a customised logo which was used on the cake, doormat, signage, cushions, bar menus, shimmer walls, casino fun money, drink toppers, and even light projections on the house. I can't tell you how many people came up to me on the night and complimented us on all the details that had gone into the event. It was 100% noticed!

- As part of your branding, you could create an event #hashtag that you encourage your guests to use on their social media. This is an easy and fun way of collecting photos from the night. After the event, you'll be able to search the #hashtag and see all the photos everyone has taken. To view some of our favourite event photos, just follow #extraordinaryparties.

3) Get your guests involved

The more you can make your guests feel like a part of your event, the more their excitement builds! They will definitely remember your event and what they did to create the magic. Here are some ideas for getting guests involved.

- Start with a dress code for your event to get guests thinking about what to wear well before the day itself. Some fun dress code examples include:
- White Party - all your guests dress in white
- Denim & Diamonds Party - guests dress in denim & sparkles
- Fifties Party - poodle skirts and high ponytails for the ladies, black leather jackets with white tee shirts and cuffed jeans for the men
- Create opportunities for audience interaction. Think about games, interactive quizzes, sing-alongs, slideshows, and speeches.

Here's a fun story about one of my favourite events where guest involvement made the evening absolutely unforgettable!

- The occasion: a 21st birthday white party for a client
- The venue: the 5-star Radisson Edwardian in Manchester
- The scene: we took over the hotel bar and transformed it

into an elite white party complete with 7 themed ice luges, including a giant ice vase adorned with flowing orchids over the top.

- The surprise: the guests performed as a flash mob to the client's favourite song, *Proud Mary*
- The pre-event preparations: we had a dance video made for guests to learn the dance
- The performance: it started with a professional dance troop. Following their first song they started with *Proud Mary*, the birthday girl was super surprised when her mum started dancing, then her auntie and a load of other guests started to join in. You couldn't recreate the shock on her face!

I saw that client the other day, 3 years after her party. We work together every year and her daughter is *still talking about* her birthday **flashmob** and her **fabulous ice party!** When we create moments like this, they will be ones we never ever forget!

You can't beat audience interaction and the impact it has on the party. I love playing games with guests! Depending on the setting and style of events, you can do this in different ways. It may be a fun interactive quiz, where guests have to guess answers to questions and have remotes on their table and have to press the right answer quickest, just like you see on TV, those fastest finger games!

I did this once for a wedding, with an upmarket version of Mr & Mrs. We had plasma screens all around the room. The sister of the bride incorporated the game into her speech. She had photos come up on the screens with questions the guests had to answer by pressing their answer choice on a keypad.

I've also done the same for charity sports quizzes - guests stood on their chairs before holding up answers to questions. At other events, everyone sang along with some incredible entertainment.

I've planned and styled 100s of events and when I look back, the ones which included elements like this really jump out for me!

Ask key people to give a speech. I do put a caveat with this one - don't ask too many people as you don't want death by speeches! I also give my clients a time window for speeches. Usually 8 minutes for the speech, plus allow 1 minute for them to get the microphone and 1 minute for them to sit down. There is nothing worse than a speech dragging on for 20 minutes! Trust me, I've had some fathers of the bride wanting to thank every single person in the room. Choose carefully, and make it meaningful.

4) Create Instagrammable moments

Everywhere we go, people are looking for the picture-perfect backdrop to snap their selfie. With Instagram having 500 million daily users (2021 statistic), many people are looking for a unique and exciting photo opportunity! So why not help them out (and make your #event a trending topic while you're at it)?

Your guests will take photos they'll keep with them forever. You get to make their experience extraordinary by providing eye candy! Maybe you'll keep it clean and simple with a unique backdrop, like a shimmer wall featuring your event logo. Or you could take elements of your theme and bring it to life with an unusual setting for your guests to revel in.

There are hundreds of creative setups you could play with. Choose one and let your wildest imagination be your guide – the more *over the top* and *out there*, the better! Incorporate a giant chair, fun props, or a feature piece.

For winter weddings, I love creating an alpine winter forest look. People pose for photos on a Central-Park-style Park bench nestled in between snow-flocked trees, with an abundance of lanterns and candlelight all around. It's pure magic.

If your guests post these photos on their socials, the memories will come up year on year in their feeds. It's like a snippet of your full event experience that they'll look back on and fondly remember for years to come. And a reminder of the special connection you share.

But... I do have to say, it's not all for the gram! Nobody wants guests to be glued to their phones. It's much more fun when the people we invatationd can put their devices away and immerse themselves in the event! Of course, there are *some moments* that will be too good not to capture.

I encourage my clients to have a videographer and photographer because we're creating one-of-a-kind events. You want to be fully present for those special moments. Bringing in professionals to document the experience is a smart choice. You'll be able to relax and enjoy the time of your life **and also** know you have amazing photos and videos to reminisce with later.

5) Entertainment

Entertainment can make or break an event; it's often the life and soul of the party! A word of caution here: some performers might look good online with great photos and websites, but it's important to know if they'll really deliver for your guests. Nowadays, it's easy to publish performance videos to YouTube, so make sure to ask for the channels or links. Check references and recommendations from people you know who have worked with an act you're considering.

I'm a huge fan of live music, musicals, and performance art. When you get the entertainment right, it can be so absolutely sensational, it gives you the tingles! I've dedicated a whole chapter of this book to entertainment because it plays such a key role in the success (and wow factor) of your event.

6) The Food - Play with your food!

As a food lover, I love to play with food at an event. Ok, I don't actually play with my food as mum would probably tell me off for not using my knife and fork properly. I mean I enjoy being creative with food. When we go to events, we don't want to eat the same kind of food we have every day.

We want food that is unique and special to the occasion, something that will challenge our taste buds. Our guests deserve cuisine that's visually attractive and creates a song and dance on the plate. Try serving food in quirky vessels or using vibrant colours that pop. You'll also find a dedicated chapter to this later on in this book - where I'll be sharing some of the most creative food ideas from all over the world.

7) Show-Stopping Decor!

The decor you choose will have one of the biggest impacts on the ambiance of your event. Along with my team at Qube Events & Productions, I style about 300 events a year. The crazier and more creative our clients allow us to be, the better the reactions from guests as they enter the room.

Decor allows you to immerse guests in a completely different world, taking them from the everyday to the extraordinary. The more effort and detail that goes into the decor, the more magic you will create. Later in this book, I'll talk you through the step-by-step of how to transform a space.

8) Create Sensory Experiences

I like to call this the sense check! Have you sense-checked your event?

This is a good way to test whether you've covered some of the key creative elements that are going to make your event truly extraordinary! Work your way through the six senses with the elements below as your guide.

As a baby grows, it learns by exploring different experiences with its senses. Baby feels comforted with your familiar appearance and scent. Baby is happiest when warm and cosy. A lullaby soothes baby to sleep and being hungry is cause to sound the alarm! I remember the first time my youngest daughter Sophia tried ice cream and the shock on her little face from the surprising cold! She loved it and can't get enough now.

1) Sight

2) Hearing

3) Smell

4) Taste

5) Touch

6) Movement

These sensory needs still exist when baby grows up into a party guest, no matter how tall! When it comes to live events, the sensory experience is important for all ages. Imagine if you sat aunty Denise under the air conditioning vent so she was freezing cold, she'd tell you quite a story.

First, you'll want to get the sensory basics right for your event.

Visually - You'll want it to look incredible - this comes down to the location of your venue, the surroundings, the decor, and how you style the room. Next, consider the scent of your room as you first enter. Treat guests to the fragrance of beautiful flowers or a scented candle on each table. You can even have a special unique scent created exclusively for your event!

Sounds - What sounds could you bring into your event? It could be as simple as epic musicians playing while guests arrive and entertaining throughout the night.

Imagine you're having a jungle-themed event. The room is dressed to take you into an immersive jungle forest floor. Vines and foliage trail from the ceiling, parrots fly through the air, and low fog covers the ballroom to emulate the forest floor. Beams of lighting trickle across the room. There are palm trees and realistic-looking jungle animals, including a life size elephant. The sounds of jungle animals and waterfall will certainly enhance the magical experience!

If you've got a show-stopping theme why not incorporate a theme song? Your guests will familiarise with it throughout the night. They'll eventually start joining in, especially if you keep playing it again and again. Deborah's 40th birthday was themed after the famous cabaret bar, Lio's in Ibiza, because it's one of her favourite places. The last time she went, they kept playing the song Bills - by Lunch Money Lewis! and were throwing money around. Every time the song played, all the guests got up and joined in.

So, for this party, I created some Debbie Dollars that included her event logo, her face, and some cute details about the party. It was all very tongue-in-cheek and definitely created a talking point. We played the same song at the party several times. Each time the guests interacted even more.

Taste - It's always fun at events to tease people's taste buds by trying new food combinations and flavours. You can bring the surprise element into the taste of food. E.g., You might be served an egg in an egg cup with soldiers (breaded fingers), like you had as a kid, but when you open it up, you'll discover a passion fruit mousse with shortbread fingers. You'll be coming to a chapter soon all about making food fabulous too, so I will go into that in a lot more detail.

Touch - we all love to touch right? Especially those of us who are tactile. You can incorporate different textures into your event to give your guests an immersive experience. It might be as simple as a gorgeous velour tablecloth that's so soft to touch. You could have diamantés or petals scattered on the tables that guests are subconsciously playing with when sat down for a meal. I've created quite a few events where we have had ice sculptures and the guests always want to touch them! It's all part of the experience.

Movement - Movement is the balance sense, which gives us information about our surroundings and the positions of our limbs. I like to relate this to our comfort. Are your guests going to be sat on cushioned banqueting chairs? Do you have some soft seating for those moments where we need to rest our feet from high heels? Think about furniture that allows guests to stretch their legs as they need. Also, give them the opportunity to get up and move at your event.

We don't want to be stuck at tables for hours on end. At a party such as a dinner dance, it's a great sign when guests are standing up in their chairs, singing, and swaying along to the music. Once one table gets up, often the entire room follows. A full dancefloor is another sign of a great party.

Movement, especially dancing, allows us to let go of the everyday, express ourselves, and connect to the music. Going crazy on the dance floor can lift your mood as well as reduce pain and stiffness. If you have the opportunity to get up and dance at an event, just do it.

Top Tip: When planning your event, do the sense check. Think about each of these elements and check if you have included something that appeals to each one.

9) Take-Home Souvenirs

Apart from the memories we make on the day/night of our events, it's always lovely to take home a little souvenir. They could be in a range of shapes and sizes. Many of you also might refer to these as *'favours'* but I'm not a huge fan of the word. It makes me think of old-school weddings when you'd get an organza bag filled with sugared almonds. If you know, you know!

Here's a list of some of my favourite take-home souvenirs.

Photo Magnets

These are really popular in Israel. You pretty much can't go to an Israeli wedding without having magnets on offer. How it works is a photographer roams the event taking photos of guests. The photos are produced into magnets on the spot for guests to take home.

Israelis often display these gorgeous souvenirs all over their fridges. The events and weddings they've been to are featured in their kitchens. Many photo magnets are branded with the couple's names and the date. This trend has made its way to the UK now and I'm starting to build up quite an event magnet collection on my own fridge.

Photo Booths/Magic Mirrors with Guest Books

This is probably one of the biggest take-home souvenirs from weddings and events in the UK. Photo Booths can come in all shapes and sizes, I've seen campervans, minis, open booths with quirky themed backdrops, 3D photo booths and more. At Qube Events & Productions, my luxury event decor and hire business, we own a premium photo booth with a green screen backdrop and huge interactive touch screen TV. It also comes with a fun box of props which we often change up depending on the event theme. It always goes down a hit with guests.

We produce two copies of every picture. The first copy is for the guests to take home. The other one becomes part of a beautiful guest book, with a chance for guests to write a special message for the event hosts. It's a gorgeous take-home souvenir the hosts can look back on for years to come.

It's all about the Merch!

I love a bit of event merch (merchandise), also known as event swag! Capture the memories and fun with branded clothing, t-shirts, hoodies, water bottles, notebooks, pens, pencils, all sorts! Pretty much anything can be branded these days and given to your guests as a take-home souvenir of the event.

I've seen a few quirky ways of handing out merch over the years. For one barmitzvah where the guest of honour was into fashion, we set up a clothes rail and loaded it with t-shirts (each shirt had flashing lights). We wheeled the entire thing out onto the dance floor and handed out the light-up shirts to excited kids!

I've also seen an official "Merch shop" at a barmitzvah party. A mock shop was created in the event room, full of branded merchandise that guests could choose from. Imagine recreating your favourite shop so your event-goers could come in, pick the souvenir of their choice, and take it home in a branded shopping bag with the event logo on! I've also seen this done with sweets - imagine a candy store at your event, with a full-on pick and mix put into branded sweet bags.

Crazy, right? But after all, we are talking about 'extraordinary parties.' If you had a Merch shop at your event, your guests are sure to be talking about it for years to come. I can hear the conversations now: "They only went and re-created the kids' favourite shop; it was so cool!"

Gift Bags

You could give out branded gift bags, filled with things people might find useful (rather than a bag of tat). Hand the bags out as guests are leaving. Or set one at each chair so guests find them as they are seated at tables.

One of my favourite take-homes is food. I know I'm not the only one who's ever had end-of-the-night munchies, especially after a really boozy night. Something like a 'Bacon Butty' (Barm/Sandwich, Burger - what you call it depends on where you're from), or if you're at a Jewish event, you can't go wrong with a smoked salmon and cream cheese bagel! I'm not sure what it is with Jews and bagels, but it's always a big hit.

Paper Souvenirs

Event geeks (like me) enjoy taking home paper souvenirs. It could be the menu, especially if you've designed a really cool one. At a Jewish event, consider giving out the benchers (prayer books used to say Grace after meals); these often have the menu and order of service inside the covers, which is really nice to look at. My family and I will sit down at home and get our benchers out for fun. Some of my family have benchers older than I am. What a topic of conversation - talking about what someone served for dinner at their event many years ago!

It's also nice to keep the order of ceremony books, especially ones that explain cultural weddings and all the meanings behind the rituals. Another souvenir my family collects are kippot. These are the skull caps Jewish men wear. Kippot are usually made in the theme colours and personalised with the event name inside. Sometimes hosts include a quirky message like 'Smashed it', and the couples name and date inside (very apt as part of the Jewish wedding ceremony involves the groom smashing a glass with his foot).

Since I'm frequently asked questions about my Jewish identity and traditions, I'll explain why something is done when the opportunity arises in this book. The reason why a Jewish couple breaks a glass at a wedding holds multiple meanings. Some say it represents the destruction of the Temple in Jerusalem. Others say it demonstrates that marriage holds sorrow as well as joy and is a representation of the commitment to stand by one another even in hard times.

Experience souvenirs

These are items people can take home after going through a particular experience. One example of this is having a caricaturist who draws a comical picture of each guest. Another option is a Silhouette artist (a talented person who uses a very tiny pair of scissors on a small black piece of paper) who will cut out an intricate silhouette portrait. Within minutes, it's finished and framed for the guest to take home.

Some of my favourite take-home favours are hangover kits or unusual place cards. For Dahlia's batmitzvah, they are shaped as a feather with a little hole in the top so guests can add them to their keyrings.

10) Create the Unexpected

My final tip for creating an extraordinary event is using creative touches to bring in the unexpected. By this I mean have lots of surprises at your event. This could be room reveals, or surprise guests or speeches. They could be theatrical surprises such as confetti flurries or indoor pyrotechnics. Some of my favourite surprise performers are people dressed as bushes or plants. It's so funny watching the guests' reactions when they get a little tap from a bush and when they turn round nothing is there. Fireworks at the end of the night are always exciting!

I believe events are all about the magic! Even if you only implement 1 or 2 of the ideas above, it will really make a difference to the experience that your guests have. That's where you can put the magic into the memories you are creating.

Bonus Tip

Sustainable Parties

I encourage you to be mindful of the environment when planning your party. Sustainability is also really appreciated by many guests too. Try and avoid disposable paper cups and plates and instead invest in fabulous creative party pieces that you can use again and again.

"FOOD IS ART AND ART IS FOOD"

Chapter Five

MAKING FOOD & DRINK FABULOUS

ood and drink both play a huge part in the overall experience and success of your event. The dining experience of your event is much bigger than which food items are on the menu. The hottest trend in catering right now embraces the art of food experiences! You'll want to think about how it's presented, what it's served on, the colours, the flavours, and the impact the food gives. Keeping all these aspects in mind ensures your guests will rave about the incredible food at your event.

This chapter is going to give you some ideas of how you could make your food and drink extraordinary. You'll find fun and quirky presentation ideas as well. I'll talk about how you can serve food in a stylish way. Plus, I'll share fabulous food ideas from some of the world's most famous celebrity chefs!

I'd love you to take these ideas as inspiration for your own events. You can use them for various occasions: from a cocktail party at home to a wedding reception, black tie gala, dinner party, or themed party. I've even given you fun ideas for kids' parties! I'm a foodie at heart, so I could create an entire book on this topic. In this one chapter, I'm sharing a small selection of my favourites.

EXTRAORDINARY FOOD

The hottest trend in catering right now embraces the art of food experiences. Instead of sitting down at a table and waiting for your dish to arrive, introduce your guests to more personal service with interactive food and drink trays. Unlike passive servers offering the same old hors-d'oeuvres and drinks, invatation your guests to participate in their meal and add excitement and fun to the occasion. Server-Performers can be decked out in beautiful costumes with trays to integrate with the theme of your party.

STYLISH & QUIRKY FOOD IDEAS

Canapés/Drinks Receptions

Sushi topped with Cheetos - Private Chef Rooz – California.

Sushi Belt - Just like at Yo Sushi, but have one at your event.

Mini Ice Cream cones filled with pate, egg, guacamole or other delicious fillings.

Cherry tomatoes stuffed with burrata and wild rocket pesto rosemary skewers, served from hanging bonsai trees (Jimmy Garcia catering).

Food as art (or is it art as food?): Canapés covered with mini glass cloches.

Make it mini - think of your favourite dish and turn it into mini bite size portions. Good things are better in tiny packages! Mini burgers, mini hot dogs, mini shepherd's pies, mini fish and chips, mini tacos served sat in lime wedges.

Create a cool pop art style vibe: Ditch the bowl and serve individual soups in mini soup cans, branded to suit your event (Idea courtesy of 24 Carrots Catering & Events).

Tacos and mini margaritas.

Starters

Dry ice infused cloche on individual place settings that waiters lift off.
Duck and pancakes served in bamboo steamers.
Mini individual charcuterie boards.
Ponzu marinated tuna, mango, wakame, soy emulsion and puffed rice (Idea courtesy of Feast by Ed).

Main Courses

Tagines served in traditional Moroccan tagine pots.
Individual Hanging skewers of chicken, lamb or beef.
Back to basics - take some classic meals and put a modern twist on them:
Picnic hampers with mini tabletop BBQs - The picnic hamper is filled with a selection of salads and food accompaniments. Each table is served partially cooked meats or fish, which is then cooked at the table by a nominated guest.

Desserts

Add gold leaf flakes atop your desserts to give that extra essence of luxury.
Edible chocolate flower pots with chocolate soil, basil moss, and a vanilla parfait mushroom/toadstools (Idea courtesy of Jimmy Garcia Catering).
Creative shaped - bauble dessert - perfect for events at Christmas.
Chocolate bombs, served with a jug of hot sauce to pour over them - the bomb melts in front of your eyes to reveal the contents inside.
Individual fondues with an array of stylish dips - a fun and inter-active dessert.

Buffets/Food Carts/Food Stations/Food Trucks

Street food style stations are all the rage at the moment. Stations with unique offerings are always intriguing for guests and 100% add to the vibe of the evening. They are the perfect way for your guest to enjoy a wide range of different flavours, creating an informal and relaxed dining environment. Guests are able to try lots of different combinations and many flavours they may have not tried before. Where you can get chefs creating live theatre behind the stations, it all adds to the ambience and fun! Guests love to watch, especially whilst mixing and mingling with their friends.

These could be in the form of a themed buffet station or cart. If your venue has space, you could drive in some quirky food trucks.

Here are some of my favourite ideas:

- Ramen station
- Guacamole & Taco station
- Paella Stations
- Sushi station (with chef making it live in front of you)
- Pizza van with stone oven
- Burger Bar & Hot dog stations, with all the toppings
- Oyster bar
- Charcuterie Bar
- Pie Bar
- Seafood Station on ice, with Ice sculptures
- Veggie garden salad station, designed to look like an actual garden

Dessert themed stations

You could take one food and do different variations of it for a fabulous-looking over-the-top display. Let's take this concept for a spin!

Your Lemon Dessert table could have:

- lemon mousse, lemon cake, lemon meringue pie, lemon biscuits, lemon cupcakes, lemon cake pops, lemon curd shots, etc...
- Dress it up by adding vases filled with lemons, rustic crates with galvanised stands, and freshly squeezed lemonade served in mason jars with yellow and white paper straws.

Crumble Station

This idea came from one of my favourite pop-ups at the Old Spitalfields market in London, called Humble Crumble. If you have never been to this market, it's well worth a visit and filled with every type of street food imaginable.

At a crumble station, guests choose a style of crumble (from 2 or 3 choices such as apple & blackberry or apple & rhubarb), then they select the toppings (e.g., blow-torched meringue, edible flowers, custard, or cream).

Use Cute Buffet Signs, using Chalkboards, acrylic signs, mini easels, lightboxes and neon signs to label foods.

If you're using a caterer for your event, they may have some fabulous ideas, but make sure to speak up about your favourites so they can create something that suits you. Whether it's a restaurant or a type of food you prefer, always ask the question, to see if that could be incorporated into a fun food station. Most good caterers are willing to listen to your ideas and bring them to life. I've had a client in the past who was obsessed with Krispy Kremes, so we ended up having a full-on Krispy Kreme bar at their event.

Other fun dessert ideas include:

- Donut Walls
- Chocolate Shawarma
- Pretzel Bar with different sauces you can dip into
- Popcorn station
- Macaron Towers
- Ice cream van or truck
- Donuts with syringes filled with chocolate, salted caramel and jam
- Pan Ice
- Churros station
- Ferris wheel cupcakes
- Cheese stations
- Waffle Bar
- Neon dessert wall - this is a quirky wall with space for placement of desserts, the actual wall itself changes colour throughout the event.
- Hot Chocolate Bar
- Themed Dessert Buffets
- Creative Shaped - Bauble Dessert
- Popcorn station
- Macaron Towers
- S'mores tables
- Serve desserts in edible sugar candy bowls
- Chocolate bombs served with a jug of hot sauce to pour over where the bomb melts in front of your eyes to reveal the contents inside
- Mini Fondues

QUIRKY PRESENTATION IDEAS

Have you ever heard the phrase we eat with our eyes? I'm a strong believer that the food for an event should look irresistibly good. Obviously, it needs to taste incredible and delight the taste buds. But I'm looking at the part before the food makes its way to your mouth. The world of events is changing and you want to give your guests experiences with food. Food displays full of colour, and interactive courses that appeal to multiple senses.

More than ever now, caterers are collaborating with event stylists to enhance their food displays. The goal is to create over-the-top food presentation ideas that enhance the event experience for guests.

Here are some quirky ideas:

If you're serving canapés or roaming food that is served from a tray (e.g., at a drinks reception), explore the creative possibilities for your serving trays.

Quirky Trays

- Trays made from long artificial grass with the food nestled in look fabulous.

- Acrylic trays which are hollow inside: you can fill them with decor to fit your theme.

- Log stumps

- Usherette Trays

- Slates

- Serve from a prop (e.g., a tennis racket for a sports theme). Think about your theme and what props are associated with it that you could put food in or on? Of course, you'll make sure it's nice and clean beforehand (or lined with paper or clear acrylic). Then, get ready to surprise your guests with all the quirky and unique props used as serving trays.

Themed Food Carts/Stations

One of the quirkiest food stations I ever created was for a car-themed bar mitzvah. It was a Petrol (Gas) Station Sweet Buffet. Over the buffet was an actual canopy like you find in a Petrol (Gas) Station and we named it after the bar mitzvah boy. Inside the station, we had tyres stacked at different heights with circular trays of sweets placed on top.

Can't decide on one theme? Pick all of them! Themed stations can give you the best of all worlds. Travel the world in one night.

Pick some themes you love most, or whittle down your top five favourite cuisines.

You can have Middle Eastern food, Chinese, Italian, British pub fare, and Indian cuisine throughout the venue space. It's a dream for foodies and picky people alike because there's so much to choose from. Plus, you can honour the cultural backgrounds of your guests.

Themed buffets can inspire creative decorations and creative food choices. Caterer Jimmy Garcia does this wonderfully. At their *Til Death Do Us Party*, they served "Eye Balls" Choux Buns filled with pumpkin puree, "Worms" Tomato jelly in black olive soil, "Severed Fingers" made out of pizza dough with an olive nail and red "blood" dip, and a duck liver parfait that looked like "rotten apples." Guests were definitely in for a Halloween surprise!

Food Walls

Imagine any style of wall with little holds/ledges in it for food to be served from. The possibilities are endless: from brick walls to foliage walls, sequin walls to walls with pegs for donuts, bagels, or pretzels. Wouldn't it be lovely at a wedding to have a wall adorned in an abundance of fresh florals with an amazing array of colourful desserts nestled in between the blooms?

These are a huge trend that is emerging and is only going to get bigger. We're going to see all types of walls themed to match the style of the event.

- Food trucks
- Tables don't even have to be actual tables; imagine stacked crates, hot dog carts, or even a human laid down adorned with sushi. Salads served in wheelbarrows. Contemporary food stations in Volkswagen vans are cool too.
- Use props to make the food stations look authentic and enticing, add beautiful display cards to label the menu. With so many different food stations, your guests can interact with each other and discover new dishes to try.

Ever eaten an edible balloon! Apple Strudel Balloons anyone?

Balloons are filled with helium and float on an edible tasty string. Eat it and your voice will go high and squeaky. I'm a huge fan of the company 'Lick me I'm Delicious'. They have lots of weird and wonderful ideas for events, including edible fragrances. Imagine a beautiful range of fragrance bottles. Simply you spray, sniff, lick and enjoy!

EDIBLE MIST ORBS

This is likely to be both a new and memorable experience for your guests - they'll literally taste the air! Pop a straw in your mouth, breathe in the air from the orb and guess what flavour you get. You could have bespoke flavours created for your event. Flavours could be cheesecake, strawberry, mint? So many options to choose from.

For a themed event, theming the food menu is a must. Whilst reminiscing about some of the themed events I've done in the past, I found the food menu for the car-themed barmitzvah I mentioned earlier. I had to share it with you.

It was written in the same font you would find on a car number plate.

Menu

Jump Start
Swarburu (they had shawarma)
Main Event
Lamb..ourghini with Turkey..ota and Masherati, fuelled with Greenery
Last Lap
Moocedes, Bugatti Brownie & De-Icer
Dessert
Lubricants and Mini Mints

Fun Food Idea for kids' parties

I think it's so important to serve food that you know kids like. You could make a play on the kid's name and their favourite fast-food restaurant by creating your own version of it (e.g., ZFC or Zac's Fried Chicken, instead of Kentucky Fried Chicken). You could have little popcorn boxes with ZFC and serve popcorn chicken inside with corn on the cob and beans.

To keep the kids entertained, have customised placemats made, full of games and quizzes relevant to your event, with a load of colouring pencils.

EXTRAORDINARY DRINK

An extraordinary drink service, like food, is so much more than the drinks. Let's start off with the drinks though. It's so important that you get this right, use good spirit brands and make sure you have an experienced mixologist who really knows what they are doing. I love having delicious cocktails served on arrival at an event, especially ones that are themed and reflect the events colours and style. I'm also all about what the drinks are served in too. A tiny wine glass makes me cringe. Here's some ideas of how you can serve drinks in a quirky way.

It's all about how you serve it.

- Drink from disco mirror ball cocktail cups*
- Test Tube shots
- Cocktails in Coconut & Pineapples
- Cocktails in Tiki Cups topped with a pineapple leaf
- Drink me bottles are cute for an Alice in Wonderland themed event
- Ice Luges are fun and interactive
- Imagine, for a ski themed event, a set of skis with shot glasses sat into it, choose 4 friends and all drink from the skis at the same time.
- Dry ice looks spectacular. See clouds of smoke trailing over your bar or steaming cocktails for extra special effects.
- Quirky/Coloured/Unusual shaped glassware
- Strolling champagne. Imagine a girl dressed in a giant ball gown where the skirt is made of champagne flutes.
- Champagne/Bubble walls
- Wheel barrels of beer
- Cocktails topped with Edible Flowers
- Cocktails finished with a Candy floss topper
- Use colour changing ice cubes in your drinks

- Sprig of rosemary on the glass
- Serve champagne from a Firetruck or VW campervan converted into a bar.

ADD MOCKTAILS TO THE MENU

We've seen a rising number of guests cut back on alcohol for health or personal reasons. That doesn't mean they should miss out on the fun or be stuck with pop or water all evening. As a host, you can support healthier habits and help all your guests to feel special, regardless of their consumption habits. Many traditional alcoholic cocktails can be transformed into non-alcoholic versions.

BRING THE THEATRE TO THE BAR

I love working with charismatic flair cocktail bar tenders. Expect a full-on show behind your bar with the most experienced flairers in the world. See glasses, bottles & shakes thrown up in the air whilst your bartenders create your drinks in style.

THEME THE SERVING STAFF

Every member of staff you have at your event should be in character with the theme. Choose the uniforms of waiting staff and servers wisely. I still remember the Hawaiian shirts that my mum had the waiting staff in for my batmitzvah! For DahliaFest I am having the staff in tropical hats, white t-shirts, black braces and jeans. You could have clothing branded with the event logo or custom ties in the event colour scheme.

* You can purchase these at www.qubeluxe.com

"LIFE ISN'T ABOUT
HOW MANY
BREATHS YOU TAKE,
IT'S ABOUT THOSE
MOMENTS
THAT TAKE OUR
BREATH AWAY"

MAYA ANGELOU

Chapter Six

TRANSFORMING A SPACE

ransforming a space is 100% my zone of genius! You can take me anywhere in the world and I'll be looking at a space, working out the most magical and unique way I could transform it for a wedding or party. Some people might think I'm a bit crazy, but I can literally close my eyes and imagine guests clinking glasses in the space, entertainment going crazy on a tiered stage, or a DJ playing from a balcony with fabulous details in the decor everywhere you look.

Someone told me today that they just can't visualise things. It's hard for me to imagine not seeing the full picture in my mind, but it's great to work with clients who can't visualise and then put their trust in me. It's the happy tears I love the most! Over the past few years, apart from during the Covid 19 pandemic (we won't go into that right now), I'd be styling over 300 events a year. Many of them are weddings and parties.

When clients come to me, we'll sit down with a blank piece of paper and design the look and feel of their entire day. Those blank sheets of paper will be filled with drawings of lavish ceremony aisles, table centrepieces, feature pieces, and more. I'm not the best artist in the world so it often looks like a 5-year-old has drawn my sketches, but my clients seem to get the gist of what I've created. Equally important, my incredible team have learnt to decipher my hieroglyphics.

Many of my largest events start with my scribbles, which often turn into visuals on the computer, and hundreds come to life every year. It's incredible to look back and think I designed that wedding or party. It all came out of my head and then my team and I created the most magical settings for so many people.

There are countless decorating options to make your event special. I could write an entire book on this one topic, so I am just going to give you a flavour of some things you might want to consider. If you would like to see photos and videos of some of my events, go and check out the Instagram of my luxury decor company

www.instagram.com/qubeevents or visit

www.instagram.com/debbiesmarks.

My first tip when designing your venue is to put yourself in the shoes of your guests. Imagine you're walking into your venue for the first time. What's the route like as you approach the front door? Could it be lined with lighting, cute signage, or a driveway lined with lanterns? As your guests enter, a well-placed welcome sign - designed to match the theme of your event - will put them in the party mood.

What sort of fabulous entrance will greet your guests? I love creating fabulous florals around doorways, themed entrances adorned with lavish drapes, or flambeaux (the official name for giant tall firepits) flanking the door. A grand event might even have a **grand entrance,** complete with a red carpet and velvet rope. If your event is at night, you could light up the building or marquee of your venue.

You can have a lot of fun with lighting! For outdoor settings, highlight trees and foliage with professional outdoor lighting (I wouldn't recommend doing any of this yourself as it can be quite complex). If you must DIY outdoor lighting, try simple solutions. I recommend fairy lights in bushes, lining your driveway with lanterns, and small light-up balls that colour change dotted all around the garden. To take your lighting next level, you could project the logo of your event onto the ground or exterior of your venue. It's even possible to pixel map an entire image of someone's face (or any image in fact) onto the building!

If your guests will be bringing **gifts,** set up a present table, including a quirky post box to hold their cards. Add some decor to match the rest of your event, usually some candles and fresh petal scatter, or maybe some beautiful rose heads dotted across the table.

Many events will have spaces for **drinks receptions**. How will yours look? This area could be left quite plain, but not for an extraordinary party! Carry your epic decor throughout your entire space from the moment you step through the door.

Think about the practicalities of this space. What are your guests going to do during this time? Usually, they'll mix and mingle with other guests while enjoying hors-d'oeuvres and drinks. This is a perfect opportunity to set up a photo booth or selfie backdrop, as well. If a dinner course is next, they'll need a spot to find their table assignments before sitting down to eat.

We need somewhere for guests to set their drinks down on. One option: tall poseur tables (tall tables), often with different coloured cloths to match your theme. A more creative choice is a modern geometric poseur table with a marble top, adorned with flowers and lights.

You'll need somewhere for guests to sit, especially if you have some elderly guests - people like to have somewhere to perch so it might be some casual seating, or chill out furniture as I like to call it, or some quirky stools for your poseur tables. You could even make a feature of the stools (e.g., for a jungle-themed event, the base of the stools could look like the legs of animals: cheetah, elephant, zebra, etc.)

The bar is a very important factor for most events. Never underestimate the effect of an eye-catching bar. Imagine this focal point – a sexy circular mirrored bar with a mega floral chandelier hanging over the top! You could even have the bar branded to match your theme or have your logo on it.

The seating plan!! Why settle for a piece of card on an easel? I'm talking about a mega feature table plan - one that looks so good your guests will want to have photos with it!

Table plans can be as creative as giant mirrors or 6ft tall feature table plans adorned with florals. My personal favourite is a 12ft freestanding tree with a massive floral canopy. Hanging from the canopy are cards with guests' names and their table plans.

You can adapt this concept for your event in a practical way. First, check that your tree will fit under the ceiling height of your venue. Next, organise the cards so guests can easily find their names - you don't want 200 individual cards hanging up.

For large events, aim for no more than 26 cards: one for each letter of the alphabet. Each card has a list of guests grouped together by surname. Guests locate their names on the cards - table numbers are noted beside each name. If you've only got a small number of tables, you can have one card for each table with guests' names listed beneath.

DRESSING YOUR PRINCIPAL SPACE

Room Layouts

The layout of the room is critical for large events. You need space for people to stand, sit, walk, mingle, and dance. It should be easy for both guests and staff to move about. I've created a few visuals of layout ideas for larger events. These can be adapted to suit the particular details of your venue or scaled down for smaller events. There are 100's of combinations you could choose from, however here's a little bit of inspiration.

Layout ideas for standing parties/drinks receptions

Layout ideas for weddings/gala dinner events with a seated meal.

The layout across was for a wedding with 116 guests:

Everything is focused around the dancefloor as this is where the speeches will be taking place and there is a live band playing all night. The top table is central so that all guests can see them and they have a great view of the stage for the speeches. Tables 6 and 7 are where the closest family will sit, one table for each side of the family. The bride and groom's friends have also been positioned closest to the dance floor.

I have labeled each table with how many guests will be sitting around it. The term 'pax' is an industry short term for capacity. I would typically use a plan like this to give to my suppliers, especially the venue, so they know how to lay the room out and where I want the tables to be positioned. I would also give it to the caterer so they know how many place settings to put on each table. At this event they had the drinks reception (cocktail hour) in a different room.

Below is a floor plan from a 60th Wedding anniversary party that took place in a marquee in one of our client's gardens. They had the reception area (cocktail hour) inside the marquee, which was dressed with 6ft light up letters spelling their names. There was a circular mirrored bar with a giant foliage chandelier hanging above it, cascading mirror balls and a silver shimmer wall backdrop for photos. At the back of the marquee, we had a dedicated space for storage, a custom-built kitchen for the event and a green room for performers.

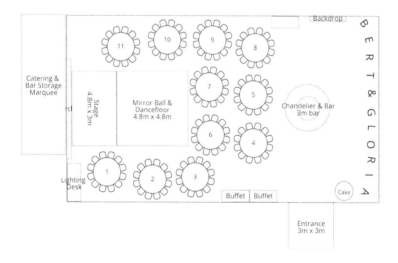

I encourage you to consider **extraordinary layouts** for your extraordinary parties and events. I absolutely love being creative when it comes to the design of a room. The layout you choose for your tables allows you to dictate the fabulousness of the decor, too. Below is a prime example.

This was a layout I created for an Indian wedding. We had 4 feature island tables, with a giant 12ft tree in the centre. From the tree extended 4 runs of long trestle tables. Please note, you need a really large space to create this look. I was working in a marquee for this event that felt like the size of a football pitch! The long tables allowed us to run decor down their centres. The round tables allowed for designs that complimented the big trees. We even had foliage chandeliers hanging from the ceiling.

The design below creates a dramatic elegant feel for any event. This is ideal for a super elegant wedding that wants to add some drama. The long lines of symmetrical tables look fabulous and you can fit large numbers into a room with a layout like this.

I've added a carpeted walkway (which I know I'd love to line with lush florals either side) down the centre of the room. The bride and groom could make a dramatic entrance walking down to the dance floor for their first dance, or to cut their cake if it was located in the centre of the dancefloor from the start.

When planning your layout, always consider the opportunity for photos. Think about where you are locating your top table and what's behind it. An ugly wall can be dressed up with a backdrop. The design below allows for plenty of beautiful florals running down the centre of the tables and lots of candles.

The next layout design incorporates striking serpentine tables. These beautiful waved tables are always a show stopper. You have to hire in this type of table because a venue won't have them in-house. Below is an example of how you could incorporate these unique tables into your design.

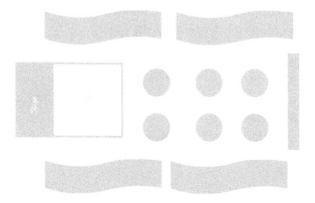

The Transformation!

When you first see your space for the first time, take a good look around and **notice everything**.

- What are the **carpets** like? *Side note: I still shudder remembering some of the hideous hotel ballroom carpets I've seen over the years.*
- Do the **walls** have unsightly wall hangings or photos?
- Notice the **ceilings**, how high are they? Do they allow for tall centrepieces, large lighting rigs, ceiling pieces, etc.? Can you make a feature of the ceiling?
- Also note the locations of **fire exits** and **doors** that you need to keep clear.

Once you've familiarised yourself with your space, the fun (decor) can begin!

Let's start with the floor. Are you happy with the carpet or do you want to cover it? It's possible to completely re-carpet or re-floor an entire space to make it unique. While this can be quite costly, it definitely makes a huge impact! Think about how much of the carpet you will actually see once everything is in place (e.g., dancefloors, tables, DJ stands, etc. . . .).

The walls. Draping the walls can create a mega feature for your event and it completely transforms the space.

Imagine the possibilities:

- gorgeous pleated white drape that absorbs lighting around the room
- black star cloth (black with twinkly lights)
- luxurious crushed velvet draping for the entire room (so opulent!)

For draping on a grand scale, I wouldn't recommend doing it yourself. Most venues won't allow you to secure drapes (or anything else) directly onto the walls. Draping is usually hung from *professional freestanding hanging systems*, often referred to as pipe and drape. Save yourself the headache and hire specialists to do this for you.

Ceiling Decor

First determine what the ceiling is like. Notice the height and if there are ceiling features you can use to enhance the decor. For example, if your venue has gorgeous wooden beams - they could be wrapped in fairy lights or you could hang beautiful florals from them.

Does your ceiling have hanging points? You might not know exactly what to look for here as these can often be hidden - ask the venue and they can advise. If you're planning to fill the room with beautiful lighting effects, your lighting company needs to attach trusses to the ceiling with special hanging points that can hold the weight of all the light fittings.

If your room has tall ceilings, you could also hang feature chandeliers (e.g., crystal, fibre optic, or even mega floral). One of my favourite chandelier installations was for a Greek wedding held at the Titanic Hotel in Liverpool (named after the famous "unsinkable" ship). We created a 5-meter-wide floral chandelier with a 3-meter-wide chandelier inside, and then a smaller crystal chandelier inside that! It was pretty special!

Ledges, Window Sills, & Alcoves

Have a look around your space and notice all the nooks and crannies that can enhance your venue. Think about how you can turn these into features. For example, a large fireplace behind your wedding table could be filled with an abundance of candles and florals.

My team often stages events in a particular castle. It has some gorgeous features that we love to work with. We create a lot of lavish ceremonies in the grand hall of the castle, where there are 3 alcoves in the brickwork of the building. We fill these alcoves with tall cylindrical vases, floating candles in water, tea lights, fresh flower heads and petals. The castle has another alcove which is the perfect spot for a photo booth.

LIGHTING DE-MYSTIFIED

This can be one of the most underestimated features of your venue. When done properly, lighting can completely transform your space and create an atmosphere like no other. I'd always recommend working with a professional lighting team to create your desired look. When you receive a quote from a lighting company, you might feel intimidated by a long list of technical jargon. Don't worry - I'm going to talk you through some of the key lighting features you could have in your room, in plain English, so you know what to ask for.

Here is my mini crash course on event lighting types and the effects they create.

Uplighters

These are one of the most cost-effective ways to transform a space. If you're only going to have minimal lighting for your event, uplighters are my top recommendation. These are small fixtures that sit on the floor and shine a beam of light up onto the wall of your space. Options include colour-changing or one colour, wired or wireless. Choose wireless uplighters to avoid unsightly wires around the edges of your room.

Feature Lighting

The 2 types of lighting described below are something you could do yourself on a small scale. If your event is on a larger scale (especially with high ceilings), I recommend hiring a professional to install it for you.

Fairy Lights

Come in various forms and are a lovely way to add twinkle to your event. They're so versatile! You can wrap them around a column, have a wall covered in fairy lights from top to bottom, wrap vertical beams in them, or string them across the ceilings of your room.

Festoon Lighting

Is ideal for more relaxed events. The best way to describe them is strings of mini light up golf balls. Festoon lights give more of a rustic, outdoor, quirky vibe. They're also great for lining walkways or driveways.

Room Wash

This could also be called a colour wash. Basically, you project a wash of light over your space. To create special effects, you can use a combination of different colours or enhance them with a haze (see below regarding haze). These lights are usually suspended from a truss mounted to the ceiling or from free standing truss systems.

Break up Gobos (pronounced 'Go-bow')

Break up what? This term refers to a small, stencilled, circular disc, cut into a pattern, shape or logo. The disc is inserted into lighting fixtures to create a projected image or pattern. Most lighting companies have standard gobos. You could also have custom gobos made for the event to project your name or logo. Gobos can be used in creative capacities (i.e., projecting a wave pattern with blue lights for an underwater themed event - your dance floor transforms into the sea).

Dance Floor Lighting

When you hire a professional lighting technician, that person controls the lighting system to create an atmosphere on the dance-floor throughout the night. Lighting can interact with the type of music. For example, you could have lighting programmed to enhance a particular entertainment act.

Or you can light up a key part of your event, like the first dance at a wedding. One of my favourite first dance moments was created with a 1m-wide mirror ball hung over the dance floor. As the couple danced, several spotlights shone onto the mirror ball, filling the entire room with magical twinkle effects.

Stage Lighting

Always make sure your stage is well lit. There is nothing worse than a band trying to perform in the dark. Check with your entertainment during the planning stage, as many DJ's (and some performers) will bring their own lighting.

For a premium party, allow your production company to take care of all the lighting for the entire room. Feature lighting on stages can be a creative design that adds to the overall look. The lighting style can compliment the event theme.

Table Lighting

Table lighting can be on the table *or* above it. You could have a beautifully lit centrepiece with LEDs or fairy lights. Table chandeliers add elegance.

For a more dramatic effect, you can pinspot the table. Keep the room fairly dark and then highlight the tables with sharp beams of light from above. Your guests will feel like they're in the spotlight!

Haze

A haze machine is a special effects machine that creates delicate clouds in the air to diffuse the light. I'd highly recommend having a haze machine at your event to enhance your lighting. Haze makes your lighting beams more prominent, like the big beams of light that sweep across the stage on the X Factor show.

A word of caution before you say yes to haze. You'll need to check if your venue allows it - many won't. The venue will need to isolate the fire alarms in your event space, otherwise the haze might set off the fire alarms. You want everyone to remember your event, but not because they all had to evacuate!

Working with a lighting company

Booking event lighting on a large scale can be fairly complex. Your event planner can be a tremendous help to you. Professional event planners have the experience and expertise to coordinate all the aspects of your party. They also know which types of lighting effects will achieve your desired results.

Professional lighting will be one of the larger costs for your event. You'll most likely have a hefty bill for the crew; they do the heavy lifting of light fixtures, trusses and more. Your lighting costs include specialist technicians who set everything up, install it, focus and programme all the lights to give you the ultimate look. Large trucks will transport all your lighting equipment in from the depot, so look out for a delivery and collection cost on your quote, too.

Tableware Extraordinaire

The tableware you choose to place on your table has a massive impact on the finished look. Innovative glassware and crockery can make all the difference to the overall look and is definitely one thing that will take your event from ordinary to extraordinary.

Use coloured charger plates to bring accent colours into your event and team with stylish clear or coloured glassware to compliment. If your event has gold accents add gold cutlery.

Tables & Chairs

There are different table styles you could choose from. The popular option is choosing a table that could have a tablecloth on it (i.e., a round banqueting table or a trestle table). If you're going for a more rustic theme, you might choose natural looking wooden tables that don't need tablecloths on them.

Tablecloths

The colour of your tablecloth makes a huge impact on the look and feel of your tables. Match your cloth to your event colours, both the main and accent colours (i.e., a black tablecloth with gold napkins). When it comes to choosing your tablecloths, pick your fabric wisely. Think about the textures you'll have throughout your event to bring it all together. Perhaps you'll have a chill out area with couches, complete with coloured cushions to match your event colours. You can even create branded cushions that have your event logo on them.

Choosing your chairs

Chairs can have a huge impact on creating the overall look of your event room! There are so many ways you can style a chair these days. Chair covers didn't get their own dedicated section in this book as I'm not a huge fan. I think they can look quite dated. A standard chair cover and bow makes me yawn. I'd always choose a stylish chair, which often has a similar cost to the hire of a chair cover and a sash.

Consider these chair styles:

- A chiavari chair - one of the most popular styles, it's a wooden chair that comes in different colours. Different colour seat pads are placed on top so you have nearly endless options for colour combinations.

- Louis chairs - an extremely elegant white chair with a padded seat and back. These come in different colours
- Ghost chairs - these acrylic see-through chairs create a striking effect
- There are many other chair styles, more than I have room to list here

Table Centrepieces

Centrepieces should be a huge talking point that encompasses the style of your event, whatever your theme. You could have a show-stopping fresh floral centrepiece for a wedding, an abundance of candles, or something uniquely suited to your theme.

When I first started styling events, I was always asked to come up with ideas for the centrepieces. I remember my very first one was a masquerade themed barmitzvah held at the Shakespeare Globe theatre in London. We had tall, thin, black lily vases on each table with a spray coming out the top with a mix of fabulous masks attached.

For height, go to extremes. Make the centrepieces tall enough so your guests can see across the table or low enough so they can easily see across the table. To create the best balance across the room, I recommend a mix of 2/3 tall and 1/3 low centrepieces.

Tall centrepieces look best with a base of decor around the bottom. By this I mean, candlesticks, tea lights, posies of flowers, petals etc. These are all low elements that sit around the base of your tall centerpieces. This brings a nice balance to the table.

The same advice applies to long tables. Low decorations look fabulous, especially with lots of candlelight included. It's also lovely to bring height to long tables. Spacing tall centrepieces equally along the length of the table with low arrangements in between.

DANCEFLOORS

If there's going to be dancing, a dancefloor is a must. This is often the central feature to your event. And an extraordinary event requires a dancefloor that makes a statement and acts as a focal point. So many possibilities - a black or white twinkly floor, a gloss dance floor featuring your event name or logo, even a quirky message, a statement, or a stylish pattern or printed graphic onto your floor.

STAGING

Why not make a feature out of the stage for your event's band or DJ? A stage could be multi-tiered, have curved edges, or be carpeted in various colours. The edges can also be different: mirrored, sparkly, or even branded edges! We're not talking about run-of-the-mill events here. These stages are for your extraordinary events, and all the details are part of the experience.

FEATURE PIECES

Each extraordinary event needs at least one feature piece. I'm talking about the things that are so spectacular, your guests' jaws will drop! Everyone will want to take photos with these feature pieces.

Here's a few examples of elements of your event you could create a feature piece for.

The Top Table

Most wedding receptions have a top table of sorts. Think of all the photos that will be taken here and embrace the opportunity to make this a show stopper! Florals can be draped off the table to pool on the floor. The front of the table can be lined with an abundance of candle light. Florals can be set along the floor growing up the front of your table. Another spectacular option is hanging overhead floral pieces above the table.

Feature Trees

My events company was one of the very first years ago to introduce table top trees as centrepieces. Now it's quite usual to have a giant tree on your table at an event. One clue that I'm a big fan of trees is inside my Aladdin's Cave (warehouse) of decor - you'll find virtually a forest in there!

Tree features aren't limited to tabletop trees. Imagine a giant tree in the centre of your reception area with seating all around the base! A large tree could hold your table plan, or grow majestically through the centre of your bar. You might use canopy style trees to frame doorway entrances or even over tables.

Large Light Up Letters

Make a statement with letters on a grand scale. The bigger the better! I love using 6ft letters as you can actually sit inside them for fabulous photos. You can also have giant letters filled with flowers, balloons or coloured lights.

Themed props & decor

Once you've chosen your theme, here's your chance to really embrace it. Themed props can be super fun. You can go wild with the theme and decor. This is where my creative mind goes into overdrive!

Imagine you've chosen Charlie & The Chocolate Factory as your theme. Picture how you can use themed props like the purple factory gates, giant chocolate bars and golden tickets. Candy Cane walkways through the entrance of your event, purple seating in chill out areas, tables topped with purple candelabras or sweet tower centrepieces. Go all out and have realistic-looking chocolate rivers dividing your drinks area from your dining area, with a bridge crossing from one to the other. You get the idea!

Maybe I've frazzled your brains a little with all the different options you can have for your event. Let me help you bring it to life a little. I'd love to tell you about one of my favourite themed events of all time. It's an event that took about a year in the making, but it was so special and one that I will always remember.

Side note: I'm a little gutted as the country went into lockdown because of the Covid-19 pandemic, the week before I was due to manage a second event for this client. They were supposed to have 200 guests at a Cowboy & Indian themed barmitzvah - in a tipi! I could still create this event for someone one day. It's all ready to go, on paper.

Let me tell you about the Barmitzvah of all time! This event was for one beautiful family who really appreciate giving their guests a memorable experience. They go all out to make that happen. Guests are still talking about the last one years later. I know I will never forget it.

The family are keen skiers who take an annual ski holiday. Their favourite resort is Val Di'Sere where there's an après ski spot called The Folie Douce. They have gorgeous memories from the place. For the barmitzvah party, they decided to have their own version of The Folie Douce, in their hometown, Leeds.

My team and I had our work cut out as the venue was a complete blank canvas. We transformed an empty hotel ballroom into a fabulous Ski Chalet for Sacha's Barmitzvah! Guests were sent their invitations in the form of a ski pass and lanyard, which arrived in a gorgeous blue bubble envelope filled with artificial snow! The family's surname was Lee, so we made a play on their family name and called the barmitzvah the La Barmy Fo-Lee.

As guests arrived at the hotel, a walkway lined with snow flocked trees led to the entrance of the *alpine chalet*. The roof was adorned with snow, there were snowy logs at the base, and a welcome sign at the top with Sacha's name and La Barmy Fo-Lee logo. Chalet girls greeted guests at the doors.

Guests entered a winter wonderland world that represented a ski resort. The edges of the entire room were lined with snowy flocked pine trees with logs at the base. Artificial snow and snow balls covered the floor of the ballroom. We did have to bring professional cleaners in the next day to get the snow off the floor, but the effect was well worth it!

During the cocktail hour, guests enjoyed a "ski lift" style photo booth with an alpine backdrop. An assortment of ski props (e.g., ski poles, helmets, etc...) brought the theme to life. The chalet girls also joined guests for photo fun! Throughout the cocktail area we had various alpine-themed wooden signs directing guests to a Bratwurst Bar, Sacha's Bar, and a Sparkle Glitter station.

We cladded out the hotel bar with timber to give it an authentic alpine look. There were wooden barrel poseur tables (beer keg style) throughout this space. We also created chill out seating with goatskin-style stools and benches, furry beanbags and arm chairs for a chalet vibe. There were coffee tables that looked like carved tree trunks. The Bratwurst Bar was a custom-made alpine food hut, similar to the ones you might find in the Christmas markets, with a snow-covered roof. We also had various ski props throughout this area, including skis, signs, wooden sleighs and lanterns.

We created a piste map for the table plan, which showcased where guests were going to sit. Each table was named after a different ski resort. In this area we also had a giant vodka luge in the shape of a ski slope! This went down a huge hit. During the cocktail hour we had a roaming sax player.

A floor to ceiling curtain divided the reception area from the dining space - we opened it up for the big reveal. Inside, all tables were laid out in 4 long rows, lined with benches and French weathered oak wooden chairs. On the back of the chairs were white faux fur throws. The benches were adorned with super authentic reindeer hides.

Down the centre of the wooden tables was a hessian table runner, adorned with various heights of hurricane vases filled with snow and pillar candles and sat on log slices. Other centerpieces included faux antlers and wine bottles with taper candle in the top and drippy wax down the sides. Each guest had their name carved in wood to dictate where their seat was in the room. Each table had La Folee Douce food and drink menus, too.

The stage for this event was a real feature. The Folie Douce is famous for its log cabin style fascias, with the DJ playing from a balcony. Steve, our in-house head of creations, pulled out all the stops to recreate this for our stage. We also used light up letters to spell out the Barmitzvah boy's name. Here's a little visual we created for the client during the planning stage.

The dining area had wireless uplighters all around the edge of the room to give a gorgeous amber glow to the space. We also projected some high-powered LED wash lights throughout the room and pinspotted the wooden table signs which indicated the ski resorts around the world (these were the table names).

A live band kept the party going all night. The food and bar service were fabulous and the bar staff were all dressed up in head-to-toe ski gear. We had skis with shot glasses attached. When the bell rang, guests knocked back shots off the skis. Inflatable giant white snow balls (AKA white beach balls) were flying around the dancefloor. We even had a snow machine at the end of the night. Yes, we made it snow in the room because we couldn't let the party finish in any other way.

"WE AREN'T AN INFORMATION AGE, WE ARE AN ENTERTAINMENT AGE"

TONY ROBBINS

Chapter Seven

EXTRAORDINARY ENTERTAINMENT

*a*n extraordinary party can't be extraordinary without extraordinary entertainment. This plays as important part as the food, the decor & the venue as ultimately this is what's going to keep your guests entertained throughout the night. This is one element that can make or break your event, ok so it won't break it literally but do you really want your wedding or event remembered for the dulcet tones of a singer who can't sing in tune? Or people groaning how bad the entertainment is...no you don't, you want guests loving everything minute, you want surprises, smiles, a full dancefloor and more! Entertainment could come in the form of interactive performers, musicians or entertaining activities. It's also great if you are looking to add a surprise element to your event.

So where do you start when it comes to entertainment. The first thing I would do is create an outline of timings of your event, so you know what kind of entertainment you need and you can look at how you can fit everything in. When booking entertainment you'll also going to need to give suppliers an idea of how long you need them to perform for and when. So some of you might know exactly what you're looking for, but some of you might not even know what's available… so I've broken this down for you to give you some inspiration about some of the types of entertainment that is available to book…please note this is not an exhaustive list, there is so much more..as well as custom designed entertainment & costumes to fit your event theme.

If working with an event organiser they should be able to recommend and design for you the most fabulous ideas for your event. I've got a little black book that I tend to bring out when working with my clients, it's all about connecting with some of the most incredible entertainers all over the world and I'm constantly on the lookout for the most extraordinary acts.

Here's a long list of inspiration for you.

WALKABOUT ENTERTAINMENT /SOLO PERFORMERS

Strolling acts are perfect for making sure that nobody misses out on the fun. The acts come to you and will mix and mingle with your guests. They will ensure that all your guests are part of the action.

Meet & Greet performers are always great to have at the entrance to your events. They create a really warm welcome for guests and set the scene from the start. Imagine showgirls in fabulous costumes or costumes with giant wings/themed costumes and so much more!

Stilt walkers (Dressed in spectacular costumes to suit your theme)
Fire breathers & performers
Mime artists
Caricaturists
Silhouette Artists - A silhouette artist gets a great reaction. It's a form of art extremely popular at the beginning of the 20th century. Guests have their profile cut into paper and stuck into a souvenir card for them to take home, its created in a matter of

minutes in front of their eyes. Its a really nice momento for your guest to take home.

Magician

Themed performers

Costumed Characters

Acrobats

Jugglers

Contact Jugglers

Living Statues (Again to suit your theme)

Living Hedges/Topiary (This is a performer dressed as a hedge/bush/plant and surprises guests!)

Living Tables

Living Walls (Imagine a wall of foilage/decor with hands sticking through it holding Champagne flutes)

Lookalikes eg imagine a Gordon Ramsay, Marilyn Monroe or the Queen joining your event.

Drag Queens

Paparazzi Impersonators

Mirror People (Performers dressed head to toe in mirror costumes, can also be used as dancers)

Vegas Showgirls

LED Dancing Robot

Fortune Tellar

Graffiti Artist

MUSICAL ENTERTAINMENT

Musical entertainers could be used in various scenarios, You might be hosting a dinner party and what a background singer. You might be looking for performers for a drinks reception, during a meal or to get the party started. Identify the areas you want entertainment and that's a great starting point so you can then work out which kind of performers would work well in the settings you have created.

SOLO MUSICAL PERFORMERS

Sax Player (Great roaming during drinks receptions)
Singer Guitarist
Solo Vocalist with backing tracks
Rat Pack & Swing Acts
Pianists
Harpists
Electric Violinists
Lazer Violins
Bagpipers
Medieval Musicians & Minstrels
DJ's
VJ's (Add some visual magic to your event with music and projections to compliment the music)
Celebrity Performers

GROUPS

Showbands
Wedding Bands
Soul, RnB & Motown Bands
70s, Funk & Disco Bands
Acoustic Bands
Tribute act and band
Christmas Bands
Jazz bands
Big Bands & Jazz orchestras
Gospel Choirs
Acapella Groups
Singing Waiters
Ceilidh Bands
Mariachi Bands
DJ Live

Roaming bands (Great for cocktail parties and drinks receptions)
Bandeoke (Kareoke where you are backed by a live band)

SHOWS

Uni-Bike Show
Motorbike
Fire Show
Acrobats
Breakdancers
Cheerleaders
Flash Mobs
Aerialists
LED/Glow Shows
Hula Hoop Show
Mindreaders
Freestyler Acts - Footballer, Basketballer
Comedian
Contortionist/Balancing act (This could be performed in a giant
cocktail glass, on top of a giant mirror ball or inside a giant snow
globe). A few years ago I was planning a winter wonderland style
wedding and we had a giant snowglobe in the centre of the
dancefloor as guests arrived into the room. Inside were 2 balleri-
nas, performing a balancing act, it was so magical.
Drone Show (For outdoor events)
Fireworks
Lazer Show
Aerial Champagne Servers

DANCE PERFORMERS

Belly Dancer
Can Can Girls
Bollywood Dancers

Snake Dancer
Vegas Showgirls
Ballerinas
Tap Dance act
Breakdancers/Hip Hop Show
Flamenco Dancers
Fire dancers
Musical Flashmob
Water dancers will amaze audiences with their fountain dancing.

CIRCUS/ACROBATIC ACTS

Jugglers
Glow Jugglers
Contact Jugglers
Unicylists
Silk Performers
Aerial Hoop
Aerial silks
Balancing Acts
Balancing Cube of Fire - This a unique act that sets a giant cube on fire and then the performer balances it and twirls it around and throws it in the air!

KIDS ENTERTAINMENT

Performers
Clowns
Party Entertainers
Caricaturists
Bouncy Castles
Fairground Rides
Magicians
Balloon Modellers

Themed Characters eg Storm Troopers/Cartoon Characters etc.
Bubble Artists

ACTIVITIES

Giant games eg Giant Connect 4, Giant Kerplunk, Giant Chess,
Giiant Jenga etc.
Facepainters
Glitter Artists
Fun Fair Stalls
Roaming Dinosaurs (Life like dinosaurs roaming throughout your
event)
Circus Workshops
Mobile Zoos
Party Bus
Pamper Party
Graffiti Artist
Virtual Reality Games
Arcade Machines
Inflatable Games
Graffiti Walls
Craft workshops

PHOTO ENTERTAINMENT

Photobooths
Magic Mirrors
Paparazzi Photographers

OTHER ENTERTAINMENT/ACTIVITIES

These are all experiences you can hire that can come to your
event, before considering any of these, scope out the space you
have to put them.

Mobile Casinos
Inflatable Games - Bungee Runs, Inflatable Table Football, Inflatable Assault Course
Karaoke
Wine Tasting
Archery Hire
Table Football Hire
Skittle Games Alley
Basketball nets
Air hockey
Cash grabber
Crazy Golf
Rodeo Bull/Rodeo Surf
Ball Pond Hire - Adult ball pools are extra fun!

WHAT TO LOOK OUT FOR WHEN BOOKING SUPPLIERS?

As an event planner, I've spent my entire career booking suppliers, so I wanted to share with you some of my top tips for getting this spot on. When you make your initial enquiry with a supplier, make sure that you provide them with as much information as possible so that they can provide you a quote. I can't tell you how many times people have emailed me asking me how much does it cost for a tablecentrepiece. This question is literally as long a piece of string question. These things might sound obvious, but I'm telling you from experience, SO many people forget to tell me this information. The key pieces of information any supplier will need initially will be as follows.

Your Event Date
Your Venue & Address
Your Type of Event
Estimated number of guests

As much detail as possible about what you're looking for.

Ie if you're booking a specific entertainer, what time do you want them to perform, do you have any specific costumes you want them to wear?

If your not sure what you want or if you have lots of questions, I would always recommend scheduling a call with your supplier so that you can make your requirements really clear.

If you're not sure about what you want, use this opportunity to tell the supplier/events company/entertainment agency about your event and the type of entertainment your looking for and they will advise you accordingly. I strongly recommend listening to event experts, they've most likely witnessed hundreds of events and have seen what works well.

Top Tips

Always request a quote in writing, look at suppliers testimonials, photos etc. Recommendations/referrals are always great too.

Every supplier should provide you with a contract, please make sure any specific requirements you have are in the contract/in writing with the supplier and go over these again a few weeks before your event.

Ask if there are any additional costs that you need to know about. I.e. if you are booking a band, do they come with their PA system (sound), do they come with lighting, stage etc? Many suppliers will add delivery and collection charges. Make sure they give you all the costs so that there are no hidden surprises at a later stage.

HOW TO GET THE BEST OUT OF YOUR SUPPLIERS?

I'm going to tell you now things that nobody ever tells you, but they make a huge difference! Have you ever heard the term, 'Happy Wife, Happy Life?' same applies to your suppliers. Happy suppliers will go above and beyond to make your event extra special, so please look after them! Think about the things they might need when they arrive at your venue, do they have a green room (somewhere to chillout) and leave their belongings whilst performing. What's the temperature like in the room they will be in, is it too hot or cold, is their soft seating for them to relax? All these simple things will make your suppliers feel more relaxed and welcomed when they arrive.

Many suppliers will also appreciate a long mirror in the chill out room so they can check they look the part before going on stage. Providing refreshments, snacks & a hot meal will also go a long way too. A lot of suppliers especially bands or entertainers at your event for a long period of time will expect a hot meal so make sure that you check how many people they will be bringing, eg if you book a band, they also might come with a sound technician who will also need feeding. I tend to call these meals crew meals. Ask your suppliers to confirm how many people they will be bringing and let your caterer know how many crew meals to provide. Your caterer should provide a cheaper crew meal option than what your guests are having, remember to ask your suppliers for any dietary requirements. If you are having an event at home and are providing the food yourself just remember to take your suppliers into consideration.

In order to make the journey easy for them to the venue, make sure you give clear directions. If your event is in a specific room, let them know, if there are special instructions for getting into the venue before it's open to the general public let them know. I'd always advise giving them a mobile number for someone onsite to contact should they have any problems and always make sure you have their mobile number too.

When you greet your suppliers, the more you can make them feel welcome and show your really excited for their performance the better. Performers thrive off the reaction they get from their audience, so starting from the moment you meet goes a long way.

 "All professional performers are extraordinary in their own uniquely talented way"

Says Nicole Geddes at Manic Stage Productions who supplies 'pop up' cirque style entertainment. Her advice to finding the exact entertainer that adds the perfect wow factor to enhance your event is to ask the experts. Take the guess work out of finding the performer that's right for you by taking advantage of the many agencies that will assist you with bringing your creative ideas to life.

Looking out for a personal approach can be key. An in person service in this busy fast paced online world of automation is hard to find. But for seamless entertainment success it's best to sit with someone who simply takes the time to sit down with you, to get creative, understand your needs, ideas and theme. This can really make a difference.. You will feel comfortable and confident in their important party of your special event before, during and after. I couldn't agree more with Nicole, having someone that really gets to know you and your requirements is so important.

"THE FONDEST MEMORIES ARE MADE GATHERED AROUND THE TABLE"

Chapter Eight

ENTERTAINING AT HOME

How to throw an epic Dinner Party

*Y*ou're planning a dinner party (or by the time you finish this chapter, you'll want to throw one). I'm so excited for you! Just call me your *dinner party fairy godmother* because I'm going to take you **step by step** through **everything** you need to do to create a fabulous dinner party.

First, take a deep breath. Yes, I'm giving you tons of ideas, but please know, it's **your** home, **your** guests, and **your** own version of a great time. Just go with the flow and have fun with it! My tip for keeping your cool is to make lists and do as much in advance as possible. List out each element you need to prepare and then work your way through it, step by step.

The key ingredients for a fabulous dinner party are:

**FOOD - DRINK - FRIENDS
GOOD CONVERSATION - DECOR**

In this chapter, we'll explore the history of dinner parties. We'll learn lessons from dinner parties of old. You might discover a tradition you love and decide to adapt it for the modern day.

Dinner parties are back, big time! After pandemic lockdowns and social distancing, we're ready to invite guests into the warm and cozy homes we've created. A night in with friends is quickly starting to become the new out.

I'm going to show you how to:

1. Style the perfect dinner table
2. Choose the perfect menu
3. Look like a wine connoisseur
4. Delight your guests with dinner party table games
5. Host a hassle-free dinner party & avoid the washing up

I'm dedicating this chapter to my Grandma Audrey, the ultimate hostess with the mostess. I have such fond memories of Grandma's dinner parties. Most of our dinner (or lunch) parties were for Jewish holidays and celebrations. We also enjoyed a traditional Friday night *Shabbat* dinner with all the family, a weekly tradition I've carried into my own home. This is the one time every week I know my family is going to sit together and talk around a table.

Grandma had what felt like the longest extending table ever - I'm sure there were at least 20 people seated at each meal. She always laid the table about 4 days or more before guests arrived. Food was often prepared weeks in advance and frozen ahead of the big day. We haven't been around the table together since the pandemic started, but I'm hoping that day will come again soon.

The first time I ever hosted a dinner party, I was laying the table and started thinking about how my grandma would present it. Everything grew from there! My dining room table decor has become more elaborate since I entered the creative event world, especially with the launch of my Qube Luxe brand, which is all about making the art of entertaining easy (more about that later). I now have collections of decor in my house. I even made myself a little entertaining room to store all my decor pieces in.

Each week, my kids and I have fun designing our dining room table. We have a range of different colour tablecloths to choose from, plus several styles of candlesticks, votives, placemats, charger plates, and more! I've started a new tradition that my entire family really enjoys, especially when we make it seasonal. It's not unheard of to have foliage runners, mini toadstools, reindeer or pumpkins on the table.

Before I go into details of how to host an epic dinner party, let's pay homage to its history. The dinner party is far from a new trend. It has ancient roots going as far back as the Greeks and the Romans, who held massive banquets with dozens of guests. It all goes back to massive gatherings with an expectation that there will be substantial amounts of food served as courses.

I wanted to share some of history's extraordinary dinner parties with you. Many of these were inspired by an article in *The Independent* written by Ed Caesar, *Great Stories That Need to be Told*. Will your dinner table be making history? Here's some pretty eventful ones.

Dinner Party with the Greeks...

For the wealthy and elite members of ancient Greek society, dinner parties were particularly luxurious soirees. At dinner parties, guests would recline on three large couches placed in a U-shape in a dining room called a *triclinium*. There, they would recline and prop themselves on pillows in order to eat, drink wine, and converse with one another.

Dinner Party with the Romans….

NERO'S ULTIMATE ORGY, ROME, AD64

The Romans were fond of a slap-up dinner, preferably one that involved gluttonous excess and lashings of promiscuity. But, according to the historian Tacitus, one banquet - organised by Tigellinus for his deviant emperor, Nero, AD64 - stands out as the most "prodigal and notorious" of the lot.

In Book V of The Annals, Tacitus writes that "the entertainment took place on a raft constructed on Marcus Agrippa's Lake. It was towed by other vessels, with gold and ivory fittings. Their rowers were degenerates, assorted according to age and vice."

Although Tacitus' recollection of the event does not extend to a menu card (there are, however, details of eye-watering sexual feats), we may assume the feast ran along the lines of the one mapped out by Petronius in his Satyricon. At that banquet, guests were treated to dormice sprinkled with poppyseed; sow's udders; a hare with wings attached, to represent Pegasus; a calf boiled whole and wearing a helmet; and more than 50 other Roman delicacies. (Yum… not!)

Dinner Party with the Tudors…

During the Tudor period and reign of Henry V, meals were not just about eating. They were a display of the monarch's power. Exotic foods demonstrated wealth, while seating arrangements reflected the court's hierarchy. The variety of food available at court was staggering. Royal diners ate citrus fruit, almonds and olive oil from the Mediterranean. Food was sweetened with sugar from Cyprus and seasoned with spices from China, Africa and India. Oxford lecturer Thomas Starkey said,

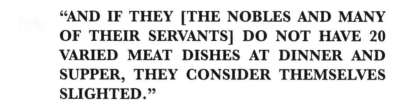

Dinner Party in the 17th Century...

NICOLAS FOUQUET'S FÊTE WORSE THAN DEATH,

Vaux-le-Vicomte, 17 August 1661

Nicolas Fouquet, finance minister to Louis XIV, had not only enjoyed a stellar career at the court of the capricious French king, but also bought himself a glorious estate at Vaux-le-Vicomte. There, he developed the greatest chateau in France. So sumptuous were the grounds, and so generous was its host, the castle became a centre for society dandies and great artists. But the fun had to stop eventually. On 17 August 1661, Fouquet threw such a lavish banquet that he was arrested. To celebrate the inauguration of the chateau, a play by Molière called Les Fâcheux (The Bores) was performed before thousands of guests who were determined to be anything but the title of the drama. Then Vatel, the highly strung chef who created Chantilly cream and killed himself when he was unable to provide fresh fish for the king's dinner, made a sumptuous, dairy-heavy feast. Fireworks marked the end of the meal, but there were more to come: Fouquet's party had been deemed too ostentatious by the king, who inferred a misappropriation of the Crown's money. Fouquet was arrested and later imprisoned for life. His wife was then exiled, and his beloved chateau was taken away from him. All this for holding the greatest shindig of the 17th century.

Dinner Party in the 18th Century...

THE REGENT'S BANQUET, BRIGHTON, 18 JANUARY 1817

The Prince Regent - later George IV of England - was such a glutton that it was said his uncorseted belly hung between his knees. No doubt he had a special place in his cholesterol-saturated heart for the greatest knees-up of his Regency: the "Regent's Banquet" at the Royal Pavilion in Brighton.

On 18 January 1817, George invatationd the greatest (and most expensive) chef in the world, Marie-Antoine Carême, to prepare a unique and extravagant dinner in honour of the visiting Grand Duke Nicholas of Russia. Carême had previously cooked for Napoleon, the Rothschilds and the Tsar. But on that cold night in 1817, Carême outdid all his previous achievements - creating 127 dishes. The evening's pièce de résistance was a 4ft-high Turkish mosque constructed entirely out of marzipan, although there were also pigeon pies, saddles of lamb and a hundred other delicacies. So pleasurable was the feast that the Prince Regent exclaimed: "It is wonderful to be back in Brighton where I am truly loved."

Dinner with the Victorians...

And then came the fancy silverware: "The Victorians added a lot of specialty tableware to their dinner parties, as part of the many, and often subtle, social norms that dictated who was part of the group — and who was not," Skinner says, a culinary historian. "Things like special lettuce and pickle forks, for example, as well as separate plates for every single possible food, specialty glass-ware, different spoons for every course."

THE FEAST OF BEASTS, Paris, 31 December 1870

On New Year's Eve 1870, at Noel Peter's restaurant in Paris, Monsieur Bonvalet, the mayor of the third arrondissement, arranged the ultimate carnivore's party for 20 of his friends. It was, you might have thought, an odd time to throw a celebratory dinner - Paris had been under siege from the Germans for months and food was scarce in the capital.

Nevertheless, Bonvalet, using his connections at the local zoo, designed an innovative menu. Guests were treated to such unusual fare as escalope d'elephant with a shallot sauce and roast bear à la sauce Toussenel. It was, according to reports, a roaring success - proof, for Bonvalet at least, that if the siege of Paris continued much longer, the poor could be fed using animals from the zoo. There are no reports, though, to suggest that Bonvalet's bold solution to Paris's food shortage was ever put to the test. The city fell to the advancing Germans on 28 January. One can only assume that Bonvalet and his friends were eating elephant casserole all January.

More recently, there was a shift toward dining rooms in the home for smaller, more intimate dinner parties — and they were also a sign of wealth: "The permanent dining room set, as we know it, didn't appear until the Early Modern period. Dining sets gradually became smaller, as wealthy folks favored more intimate gatherings and as shifts in economics meant that the middling classes could also afford a home with a small room (rather than a great hall) dedicated to eating."

By the mid-century period, that era of housewives throwing glamorous dinner parties, the precedent had long been established. As the post-war economy boomed and the middle class grew, it became increasingly more common for people to entertain guests in their homes, and that period of prosperity brought with it "an expectation that the food will be pretty substantial and that it most likely will be served in courses," Skinner said.

As the dinner party evolved throughout modern history, the ability to throw a lavish dinner party definitely became a signifier of class status. Hosting a dinner party required having a home big enough to host gatherings and comfortably seat people at a dinner table, the money to supply guests with several courses of food and alcohol, the time to prepare elaborate meals, and the disposable income to furnish your home with sets of formal dinnerware, stemware, candles, table decor, and all the other trappings of formal dinner parties. Having a dinner party was a way to show off your extensive social connections, your wealth, your place in society. It was a sign of having good taste.

It's safe to say the dinner party has continued to evolve further everyday. I've taken a good look at dinner parties in the 60s and compared them to where we are at today. Even though telephones were fully functional 60 years ago, entertaining looked very different to what it does now. **_Good Housekeeping_** magazine reported some of the trends 60 years ago. When looked at from a modern perspective, some of these are total no-no's, others are still going strong, and a few have lapsed that I think should definitely make a comeback!

Here are some ideas and inspiration for your dinner party.

Dinner Parties in the 60s... Dinner Parties Now

In the 60's	Now
It was considered poor taste to extend an invitation any way other than by mail – which also guaranteed invitations were sent far in advance.	Dinner party invites often come in the form of a WhatsApp message, or whats app group. I actually love whipping up a quick invite on Canva and sending it to my friends.
The guest list was carefully curated. Parties were not just a way to socialize, but a way to fulfill obligations to acquaintances or colleagues. Guest lists were carefully combed over to include the most interesting guests who would enjoy *each other*. According to *The Calvert Party Encyclopedia,* hosts should: "... blend a group which will enjoy each other's company and make for a pleasurable evening."	These days, we are often hosting intimate dinner parties with our closest friends and family, especially when it comes to seasonal celebrations. Some of the best conversations are had around the dinner table, so I'd encourage us all to host more dinner parties and use them as networking opportunities.
The host always greeted guests at the door. The host's job was to guide the guests through the party from start to finish, from greeting them at the door to saying goodbye to them at the door.	I still do this today; my guests are usually greeted with a big hug from me!
Seating arrangements were crucial. Some parties were more free-form, but if you had a formal dinner party, place cards were a must. For a great party, it was up to the host to seat their guests next to people they would have something in common with to talk about.	I like hosting dinner parties with place cards, but I do admit they don't always make an appearance. When I do have place cards, I like to tie it into the theme (i.e., place names sat into pine cones for an autumn table, or star shaped place names for New Years eve dinner parties).

Dress codes were important. No one wants to show up to an occasion over- or under-dressed. So, no matter the kind of event — from casual backyard gatherings to family-friendly birthday parties — including the dress code on the invite was very common. A lot of parties were formal. People dusted off their jewels and dressed up for parties back in the day. From formal black-tie dinners to cocktail soirées, partygoers were dressed to the nines.	Modern day dinner parties are often "dress as you like." If you're hosting a themed party, then the dress code should 100% go onto the invite. You might want to go all out and create a black-tie dinner party in your home. It's not something guests will get an invite to do often, but it will definitely mean a very special night will be in order. You might host a murder mystery dinner party and have guests dress up in character, or host a denim & diamonds party with jeans as the dress code. I really think these days anything goes. You have the privilege to set the tone of the night by telling guests what the dress code will be.
People brought out their fine china. Again, it wasn't just your good friends that you'd entertain at these parties, but people you wanted to impress. So, hosts would often polish their silver and bring out the fine china when hosting.	Today dressing the table as a host is done to create an experience for our guests. We want to create a look we are proud of. I have my "good set" of plates, glassware and cutlery that went on my wedding list, but these days, I like to mix it up and make my tables more eclectic and creative.
Flower arrangements were a must. Every host knows that a floral centerpiece is the key to a tablescape. No one would be caught entertaining without a dramatic floral arrangement or greenery moment.	Today, we still love a centerpiece, but often it's more candlelit than floral, or a mix of both. It's important to not make the centerpieces too tall or we won't be able to see our guests on the other side of the table. There is definitely a modern trend which sees beautiful decor running the full length of our tables.

	up a dish you've worked hard to create. My husband enjoys cooking. I asked him how he feels when guests sit down at a table and tuck in to his dishes. He said he feels happy, relieved it came out well, and a sense of achievement.
Guests never helped themselves to a drink. It would be considered rude if a guest helped themselves to the bar upon arrival, as it was the host's responsibility. Drinks were typically made in the kitchen or bar, then brought out to everyone.	We are definitely more of a help yourself generation. If you want to make your party a little more formal, you can prepare cocktails or champagne to greet your guests. Simple touches like this give your parties that sense of finesse. Drinks trolleys in our homes are on trend. As the hosts, it's gracious to make a drink for your guests.
But the punch bowl was fair game. Punch bowls made things easier on the host, as they could make a large serving and leave cups out for guests to help themselves. Just use caution: The punch was typically deadly.	I'm more tempted now to have a stylish punch bowl, (e.g., a luxurious silver stag with antlers and a punch bowl in between that can be filled with ice and bottles of your favourite bubbly).
Kids didn't eat with the adults. Kids weren't often on the guest list at dinner parties back in the day. Instead, their dinner would be served before guests arrived and they would be sent to their bedrooms to play. Or, if they were invited, they sat at the kids' table.	Not much has changed here. There's something great about kids-free adult dinner parties, ones where you can have deep and meaningful conversations without having your little ones nagging you every 2 seconds. There is a time and place for these kinds of dinner parties. Family/friends parties where kids are invited are also special. A kids table is always good, especially if you can give them games/activities to occupy themselves.

Kids usually made an appearance before going to bed. In a very *The Sound of Music*-esque manner, kids were brought out to say hello to guests before their bedtime. You may even remember your parents doing this with you if they entertained.	I personally remember reenacting the scene from the Sound of Music on my staircase at home when I was a kid. I think it was my way of not wanting to go to bed! Entertaining can be great if you have kids, especially young ones when it might not always be easy to get a babysitter (or you're just not ready to leave them for long periods of time). Bring guests to you and have a party in your own home - problem solved.
Themed parties were also popular. As food trends pushed towards exotic cuisine in the '60s, there became a fascination with themed parties. Luaus were especially popular at the time.	I love this and I'm a huge advocate for themed parties as they are so much fun! Recently, my team styled a Club Tropicana party for one of my clients. We've created a tropical summer party and Flamingo-themed kid's party. The themed dinner party trend is an emerging one. We're going to be seeing a lot more interactive themed parties at home over the next few years.
People loved costumes. Partygoers donned all types of party costumes throughout the '50s and '60s – anything to be festive, we suppose.	We're not as good at this now as people were in the '50s & '60s. It can seem like an effort to get dressed up in a costume. Still, people have the most incredible time when they make the effort. The more we can encourage our guests to do this, the better.
Fondue nights were always a hit. As fondue grew more and more popular in the early '70s, it became the perfect way to gather your friends together for a night of cheesy goodness	We don't see this so much now. There may be a little resistance about putting your skewer back into the same pot other people have shared from. It's a fun way to entertain around a table, even if it's just a dinner party with a loved one.

	A romantic cheese and chocolate evening (not in the same pot!) with fine wines sounds like a great night.
Evenings were filled with many toasts. Toasts were a standout part of any mid-century party. It wasn't limited to just the host, so it wasn't uncommon for more than one person to raise a glass throughout the night with either a funny limerick or a sincere thanks.	I love this! What a great tradition to include (even informally), to celebrate someone's milestone birthday or a special occasion. Each person around the table tells a little story or anecdote for a meaningful and special night.
Decorations were seasonal. No matter the season, it was reflected in the decorations. A holiday party wasn't complete without some greenery or lights, while spring was dominated by floral patterns and pastels.	Yes, yes, and yes to this one! Seasonal home decor trends are bigger than ever now. This extends to our parties at home too. The tablescaping trend and done-for-you style kits make this an easy way to dress up your party.
Beer was only served one way. If you asked for a beer at a cocktail party, don't expect it to come in a bottle or can. Beer was only served in a glass — a beer glass, to be exact.	I think we can safely flip this one on its head. Even at the most luxurious parties today, beer is being served in bottles. Don't forget the lime wedge in the top of your Corona bottle!
Using the appropriate serving dishes was important, too. There was no shortage of ceremony at this time. There were items that served very specific uses (and nothing more!), such as soup dishes vs. chowder mugs.	This is still important. Serving food in a stylish way all adds to the experience. For Christmas you might serve your turkey on a beautiful stag themed platter with antlers, serve salads in stylish bowls, etc. These small details mean a lot.

Cigarettes were offered to guests. As most people smoked, cigarettes were usually a constant at any type of party. It was common for the host to display a cigarette case and offer it to guests throughout the night. There were also always ashtrays around. Because you didn't want ash to end up in your carpet, of course. Ashtrays were typically scattered around your house for this very reason.	This trend isn't around much today. It all depends on whose house you're in and if they're smokers themselves. If you're not a smoker, you're definitely not encouraging it.
After dinner, the music started. Whether it was a subdued gathering or a festive affair, the evening typically ended with music and dancing.	This one depends on the personality of your crowd! If you know they'd be up for it, crank the music up.
Party games were popular. From card games to charades, parlor games after dinner were a common pastime.	I love a good board game around the table with my family! This is another one that is crowd dependent. When kids are at your table, it's definitely a way to keep them entertained. Charades and jokes at the table are always fun, as are trivia nights.
Guests knew not to overstay their welcome. No one wanted to be the drab guest who couldn't get the hint. Usually, people cleared out a couple hours after dinner, just to be safe.	It's common these days for your guests to stay for hours. Maybe it's because we are all time-poor, so when we make the effort to get together, we want to make the most of it. Often the after-dinner chat is the best. If you need your guests to leave or feel they are overstaying their welcome, comments like, "I'm so tired," or "I've got an early start in the morning," will give your guests the hint.
Thank you notes were always sent to the host. Whether it was a formal dinner party or a casual backyard gathering, guests typically sent a thank you note in the mail a few days after the event to the host.	Thank you messages are still the done thing, but now more in text form! Sending your host, a little thank you card in the post would be extra special and certainly appreciated.

STYLING THE PERFECT DINNER TABLE

I could hardly wait to write this section of the book! During the Covid-19 Pandemic when we couldn't host any live events, I launched an entire business about styling your table at home. Styling your table is all about creating the ambiance for your dinner party.

There's nothing like sitting down to a beautifully laid table - and the process of setting it up is lots of fun. I love dressing my table with my daughters and seeing it all magically come together. Plus, you look forward to the **wow** factor when your guests walk through the door.

I'm going to talk you through all the key elements of your tablescape, the official name for the art of laying a stylish table. When planning your tablescape, consider the table as a whole and not just separate elements. Every little detail contributes to the overall finished look.

Here are the essential elements to creating the perfect table. The example below is for styling a Christmas table, but please note, all these same elements apply year-round, just change them up to reflect the different seasons.

A Beautiful Tablecloth

Cover your table in a stylish tablecloth. You can select from a variety of colours, motifs, and textures to enhance your theme. This is the base layer that sets the scene for the entire table as an experience. Consider a velour tablecloth (instead of linen or damask) to give your Christmas dinner a warm, holiday look.

A Table Runner

The runner is a central part of your table - it ties everything together and acts as a base to your centrepiece. Coordinate the table runner with your napkin colours and fabrics. This is a great way to add an accent pattern, a pop of contrasting colour, or a luxe texture on a smaller scale, compared to your tablecloth.

A Gorgeous Centrepiece

Start with a gorgeous glitter, berry, or pine garland. Mix in an abundance of candlesticks and votives. Of course, you'll want feature decor: perhaps an elegant wooden or ceramic reindeer or illuminated glass Christmas trees. Add twinkly lights to the centre-piece for the ultimate showstopper of a table!

Placemats

Each place setting should have a distinctive placemat that firstly demarcates each seat, and also gives your table more of a luxury edge. When guests sit at your Christmas table, it should feel different (more special) than other moments throughout the year. For seasonal dinner parties, have different colours to match the season. I love a rusty colour for the autumn, pastel colours for springtime, and vibrant colours for the summer.

Charger Plates

A tablescape is definitely not complete without a show-stopping decorative glass charger – it brings real finesse to the table. A charger plate is a large, decorative base setting on top of which other dinnerware is placed. They are merely decorative and are not meant to come in direct contact with food. Charger plates provide an elegant way to serve multiple course meals, where each course is served in a separate bowl or plate and placed on top of the charger.

Fabric Napkins

To create a luxury tablescape, you need a quality linen napkin. Paper napkins are less elegant and consume natural resources. Machine washable napkins are easy to clean and reuse again and again.

Napkin Rings or Napkin Detailing

Napkin rings are accessories that elevate your gorgeous napkins into showpieces! If you must skip the napkin rings, then find a special touch that goes onto the napkin. Cinnamon sticks, greenery, or small gifts for each guest.

Stylish Cutlery

Cutlery is one tablescape element that often gets overlooked. Don't miss the chance to create an impact with cutlery in elegant finishes and striking styles. Personally, I have silver cutlery sets that were wedding gifts. I also have a collection of cutlery in different colours and styles (e.g., antique silver lace, pink and gold, black and gold, rose gold, etc.). I can change up the cutlery to complement the rest of my tablescape.

Gorgeous Glassware

Elegant dinner experiences include drinking from a stylish glass. Your well-laid table will include loads of glassware. A red wine glass, a white wine glass and a water glass are the essentials. Consider jazzing up each place setting with an accented coloured water glass. I'd recommend certain styles of glasses for each type of wine. I'll explain later how to know which glass to use for what.

Add Festive Friends

I don't mean having your friends show up in their favourite holiday jumpers. I'm talking about adding character to your dining table in the shape of animal figurines (i.e., snowy owls, stags, Easter bunnies, reindeer, etc.). Set them all in a collection of candlesticks and florals for an eye-catching display.

Finishing Touches

These are the special features you add to make your table a talking point. For Christmas dinners, scatter the table with snow and diamantes. New Year's Eve tables look gorgeous covered in gold confetti.

Perfect Place Settings

Do you ever sit down at a table with loads of cutlery and don't know which piece to start with? When I was 16, I carried out my work experience with an international hotel chain. During this time, I ended up on a silver service course where I learnt exactly how to lay a table and silver serve. I remember silver serving my family around the table at home.

How to Create the Perfect Place Setting.

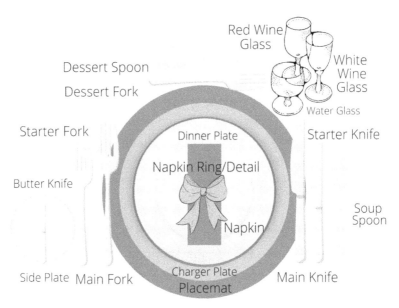

Debbie Marks guide to creating the perfect place setting

CHOOSING THE PERFECT MENU & FOOD PLANNING

Choosing a menu for your dinner party can feel daunting at first. I'm going to show you the simple steps to make it easier and more enjoyable for you. Once you have determined your guest list, check if there are any dietary requirements because this could have a big impact on what you choose for your menu (i.e., if 50% of your guests are vegan, a completely vegan menu might work best).

My biggest tip here is keep it simple. The last thing we want is a stressed-out host. The more you can prepare food ahead of your dinner party, the easier it will be. If you need to supplement a menu item or two with something store-bought, just do it. Remember, the most important thing is having everyone around the table.

When you start planning your menu, first answer the following questions:

1. How many guests are you having?
2. Do your guests have any dietary requirements?
3. Which season or special holidays are happening around the time of your dinner party? *These may influence the theme for your dinner party food and decor.*
4. How much time will you have to prepare your meal? Can you make any elements in advance or are you under time constraints on the day?

Tailor your menu around the time you have to make everything. Then schedule your dedicated time slots for cooking in your diary. Allocating your time will take away any worry about whether you will get it done or not.

"Traditional dinner party" brings to mind a traditional meal, served at a beautifully dressed table with all our finery. Dinner parties can be extraordinary too! I encourage you to think out of the box and create something weird and wonderful! Embrace the fun of a flamingo inspired luncheon or "nerd out" with a Star Wars dinner party. Whatever your theme is, it's great to tie in the menu to it where possible.

Here are a few guidelines to help you steer your menu selection in the right way.

Think about your season. - Warm weather calls for simple salads and grilled meat or fish. When there's a chill in the air, serve your guests comfort foods like heartwarming soups or a poultry/meat dish and vegetables.

Choose your main dish first and then pick starters and sides to compliment those flavours. Key dishes to think about would be for:

Starters
Mains
Sides
Desserts

Think about what ingredients can be prepared before the party and also what seasonal ingredients are available to use.

Think about offering your guests snacks or canapés on arrival. Place these on some elegant serveware for an amazing first impression. Also, you might want to buy some nice artisan breads from a local bakery for your table and serve with salted butter.

Dessert can be simple as a large pot of luxury ice cream, some beautifully cut fruit and a cheeseboard. As a huge dessert fan, I offer guests an array of different choices to sample. Guests always rave about my raspberry pavlova with chocolate (thanks to my auntie Denise, a professional chef, for the recipe).

Ideas for serving food at your dinner parties:

1. Full service: food is plated in the kitchen and served individually to guests.
2. Family style: all the food is brought to the table in serving dishes. Guests pass the dishes around the table and help themselves.
3. Mini buffet: lay all the food out nicely on a kitchen island, counter, or table. Guests walk up and serve themselves. This way guests choose what they would like most and there's less waste.

Make sure that you're fully stocked with coffee, flavoured teas, fresh mint and petit fours (these could just be a box of chocolate or some sweets) for those after dinner hot drinks. Set out a sweet bowl with lots of different styles of sweets, like a mini pic n mix (many of us are big kids at heart).

Menu Themes

I've listed theme ideas for your dinner party menus. Allow yourself to have fun with your themes. Adapt ideas to suit you and your personality. Bring creative elements in, like figurines on your table, or quirky objects for light hearted fun.

You could create an entire dining experience around your menu theme. For my birthday, my family created an Asian fusion themed dinner party for me. We sat on cushions on the floor with low tables and chopsticks, eating sushi and stir fry, and I absolutely loved it!

I asked Mike Jennings a good friend, private chef and owner of the Hospitality Hut for his advice on choosing an extraordinary menu.

 "I think it is fair to say, that whenever you are cooking at a private event you need a showstopper of a dish!

You will always be guided by the guest with regards to a menu but you almost always need a dish that makes all the guests go WOW!

This can be a Tomahawk steak with charred asparagus or even a Fruit De La Mer platter on crushed ice but one of my favourites was during a summer garden party. The party was busy with around 50 guests all getting tucked into the buffet menu and the food was going down a storm. We then served "the showstopper" at around 8:30pm when the alcohol was flowing. This was a slow cooked Moroccan spiced whole leg of Lamb served with flat breads, fiery chilli sauce, shredded lettuce, cucumber & mint yoghurt and warm flat breads. Well the guests were literally queuing around the house, literally every guest was in the queue. The feedback from the host and all the guests was incredible and we ended up picking up a lot of repeat customers that night!"

FUN DINNER PARTY MENU THEME IDEAS

Mediterranean
French Finesse
Italian Night
Greek Tavern
Asian Fusion
New York Diner
Pub-Grub/Sports Theme
Maritime (Seafood/Fish meal)
Persian theme
Moroccan Nights
Breakfast for dinner (Pyjama dinner party)
Mexican Taco Fiesta
Tapas dinner Party
Fondue Night

DINNER PARTIES & WINE

Wine is an essential ingredient for most dinner parties. From palate cleansing aperitifs to pairing wines with courses, let me show you how to bring your A game next time you have people round for dinner. I've learnt lots of tips and tricks from working around some of the best sommeliers, and I'm sharing them with you.

Years ago, I was at a vineyard in Israel learning all about different Israeli wines. I discovered there is an art of how to taste a wine, smell its aromas and really experience the wine fully. If you've never done a wine tasting before, I'd highly recommend it.

To get the most out of the wine you're opening, pour it into a glass shape that enhances its key features. When it comes to wine glasses, size and shape matter! In smaller glasses, a smaller surface area of the wine comes into contact with oxygen. Larger glasses provide more contact with oxygen, so the wine is aerated.

Wine experts have come to the conclusion that the size and shape of a wine glass can enhance the aromas, the flavour, finish of wine (the sense of texture and flavour that linger in your mouth after you have drunk it) and how it feels when the glass touches your mouth. Every wine has different characteristics and intensity, so it isn't a one size fits all situation with your wine glass selection. Although it can sound confusing at first, there's a very basic science behind it, which I'll explain. Science is fun when it involves wine!

Let me make it simple for you.

Red Wine

Serving red wine is all about letting it breathe (aerating it). The bigger the surface area for the wine in the glass, the better. The idea is to increase the time your wine is in contact with air before you start sipping, especially really fruity red and full wines. The reaction to the oxygen enables the flavours and the aromas of the wine to breathe, so all of those lovely fragrances you get from wine can be even more expressive than if they had been served in a small wine glass.

I'm sure you've seen people swirling red wine in a large glass before drinking it. Swirling gives the flavours a natural boost. If you pour wine about half an hour before you plan to serve it, it will allow more time for the wine to react to the air. Make the most of your red wine by pouring it into glasses or even from the bottle into a beautiful carafe. Remember to serve your red wine at room temperature.

Glass Recommendation: Large wide glass

White Wine

For white wine, a medium sized wine glass with a U-shaped bowl is best. White wine isn't enhanced by aeration like red wine is, so there's no need for a large glass. A rounder shape will help maintain the wine's cool temperature. Reminder: pop your white wine in the refrigerator in advance of your party, ideally a couple of hours before pouring (or 20 minutes in an ice bucket) so the bottle can cool to 7-10 degrees Celsius. Enhance your table with stylish wine buckets for your white wine bottles.

Glass Recommendation: Medium Sized U-Shape Glass

Rosé Wine

For rose wine you want to use the same style of wine glass that you use for white wine. Rosé also is best served chilled. The medium-sized glass directs the delicate floral and fruit aromas to the top.

Glass Recommendation: Medium Sized U-Shape Glass

Sparkling Wine

The famous champagne flute isn't just to make your bubbly look the part. The flute is actually a very clever design that strikes the perfect balance between containing the bubbles in the glass, whilst allowing just enough surface area to detect the wine's notes with your nose. It's a complete opposite to red wine - it's important that the surface area in the glass is small in order to minimise air contact. Otherwise, you risk the wine losing its sparkle and becoming the dreaded flat fizz.

The bubbles in sparkling wine or champagne are created as a result of carbon dioxide that has been trapped in the wine during a second round of fermentation in a sealed wine bottle. As the bubbles have nowhere to go, the pressurised environment causes the carbon dioxide to dissolve into the wine, creating a fizzy wine texture. The moment the bottle is opened and air comes into contact with the wine, the pressure is released. That's why there's a special knack to opening a bottle of bubbly - if you don't want the cork to shoot across the room, be sure to put your hand over the top of the cork when opening. It's a matter of time before bubbles start to mellow, so don't open your bottles too soon before serving.

Glass Recommendation: Flute

But how do you know how much wine to buy? How much will people drink? None of us here are psychic, but we can use this chart that writer Marissa Ross cleverly put together to predict how many glasses of wine your guests will consume, based upon the duration of your dinner party and their love of wine. Marissa is a **writer; wine columnist and humorist** and I think she's got this spot on! I told you I was going to make the process of planning events and dinner parties easy, so here you go. Your ultimate guide to how much wine people will drink.

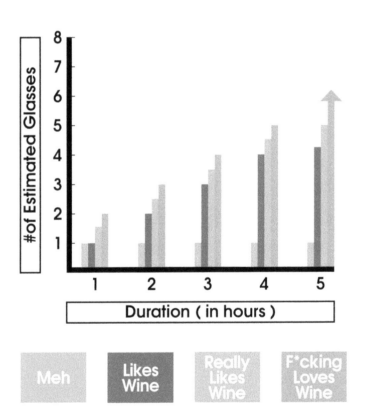

OKAY, SO *WHAT* IS THE FORMULA FOR THE NUMBER OF BOTTLES OF WINE?

Pull out your phone's calculator app (or an actual calculator) and do this.

Number of Guests × Number of Estimated Glasses Per Guest ÷ 4 = Number of Bottles Needed

And voilà! Glasses will be full, guests will be happy, and you won't run out of wine.

Top Tip: Make sure you have a good corkscrew. There is nothing worse than having wine to drink and not being able to get into the bottles.

HOW TO CHOOSE YOUR WINE FOR YOUR DINNER PARTY

As a rule of thumb, your wine should always compliment the food you are serving. You might even choose to have different wines for each course. Pairing wines with dishes enhances the flavours of both the food and the beverage.

Here are some suggestions for wines that work well with different meals.

Poultry

Chicken - Medium to full-bodied Sauvignon Blanc, Pinot Grigio, Oaked Chardonnay (White), Pinot Noir, Zinfandel, Grenache (White), Cava, Prosecco or Champagne (Sparkling)

Roast Chicken - Chardonnay

Fried Chicken - Prosecco

Turkey - Chardonnay, Pinot Gris (White), Beaujolais, Pinot Noir, Carignan (Red)

Roast Turkey - Oaked Viognier

Turkey Meatballs - Pinot Noir

Duck - Medium-bodied red such as Pinot Noir or Zinfandel

Duck breast - Pinot noir

Curried duck - Gewurztraminer

Duck a l'Orange - Beaujolais

Goose - Medium to full-bodied Nebbiolo, Gamay, Barbera (Red), Riesling, Pinot Gris, Chenin Blanc (White)

Meat

Beef - Red Wines - Cabernet Sauvignon (light to medium body and a definite crowd pleaser), Merlot is a medium red, Pinot Noir, Grenache, Tempranillo. Full bodied red, Shiraz

Steak - California Cabernet, Bordeaux, Malbec

Beef Bourguignon - Pinot Noir

Beer Stir Fry - Zinfandel

Lamb - Rioja, California Cabernet, Bordeaux

Roast Lamb - Cabernet Sauvignon

Lamb Stew - Rioja

Pork - Beaujolais, Pinot Noir, Zinfandel (Red), Riesling, Gewurztraminer, Chenin Blanc

Roast Pork Belly - Riesling

Pork Chops - Pinot Noir

Ham - Riesling, Moscato, Chenin Blanc, Rose, Lambrusco, Grenache & Zinfandel

Venison - Cotes du Rhone, Pinot Noir, Zinfandel

Tagine (Mild spiced foods) - Chilean Carmenere, Spanish Garnacha

Fish and Seafood

White Fish - Chardonnay, Chenin Blanc, Riesling, Pinot Grigio (Whites), Pinot Noir, Beaujolais, Zinfandel (Light bodied Reds)

Seabass - Riesling

Halibut - Sauvignon Blanc

Grilled Tilapia - Pinot Grigio

Tuna Steak - Pinot Noir

Swordfish - Chardonnay

Salmon - Full bodied whit wines like Chardonnay, Viognier, Marsanne, White Rioja, White Burgundy, White Pinot Noir, Beaujolais

Shellfish - Medium-full bodied whites. Muscadet, Sauvignon Blanc, Riesling, Pinot Grigio, Albarino, Gruner Veltliiner, Chardonnay or a dry crisp Champagne or Cava

Lobster - Chardonnay, Riesling, Sauvignon Blanc, Rose or Chianti

Calamari - Brut Champagne

Oysters - Muscadet

Vegetables

Mushrooms - Pinot Noir & Dolcetto (light-bodies, but full of savoury depth)

Broccoli - Chardonnay

Spinach - Sauvignon Blanc

Runner Beans - Sancerre

Parsnip - Viognier

Carrots - White Bordeaux

Onions - Beaujolais

Butternut Squash - Oaked Chardonnay

Courgettes - Dry Riesling

Pumpkin - Viognier

Lentils - Aglianico

Peas - Sauvignon Blanc

Beans - Zinfandel

Tomatoes - Albarino

Aubergine - Zinfandel

Avocado - Pinot Grigio

Roasted Asparagus - Savinniers (White wine)

Pasta

Spaghetti - Pinot Grigio, Gamay, Pinotage, Rose, Chablis.

If your spaghetti is cheese based, any light-bodied white (e.g., Chardonnay or Riesling) or red wine, pinot noir will enhance the creaminess of the cheese.

Sauces

Cheesy/Creamy Dishes - Dry rose, Pinot Grigio, Assyrtiko or Sauvignon Blanc BBQ/BBQ Sauces - Malbec, Shiraz, Cotes-du-Rhone

Lightly spiced dishes - Syrah

Pâtes, Mousses & Terrines - Zinfandel

Desserts

Chocolate Desserts - Vintage Port, Tawny Port, Cream Sherry, Pedro Ximenez, Rutherglen Muscat or Sweet white wines, Riesling, Eiswein Tokaji

Nuts - Sauvignon Blanc or Chardonnay

Fruity Desserts - Moscato d'Asti

Lemon Tart - Riesling

Apple Crumble - Gewurztraminer

Christmas Pudding - Sauternes

Cheesecake - Sauvignon Blanc

Crème Brulee - Sauternes

Cake or Cupcakes - Oaked Chardonnay

Sticky Toffee Pudding - Tawny Port

Treacle Tart - Madeira

Salted Caramel - Champagne

Soft cheeses - Moscato (White)

Cheese board/Charcuterie - Pinot Noir

Anything Salty - Champagne!

To make your wine pairings stand out at your dinner party, go for the unexpected. Consider choosing your wines from exotic regions that are unusual hot spots for wines. Plan ahead, like a great host - order some bottles in advance and try them yourself. It's all part of the research, right?

In a nutshell - pair a heavy meal with a heavy wine. Mild-tasting meals pair with mild-tasting wines. Spicy foods need spicy wines.

STRESS FREE ENTERTAINING AT HOME

Right now, you might be super excited to start planning your next dinner party. Or you might feel overwhelmed with all the ideas (and frankly, the idea of cooking and all the prep is giving you palpitations). Are you having visions of taking a burnt turkey out of the oven, or serving up dishes that all your guests will pretend to love?

There's a memorable scene in the movie *Bridget Jones Diary*, when she served up blue Leek soup. Bridget had tied the leeks together in the soup with blue string and of course the colour ran. Her blue soup recipe has now gone viral, but I know we're all hoping to avoid a similar disaster! Cooking isn't for everyone, but if you love it, embrace it and enjoy the process of all the planning.

However, you're feeling, don't worry, I have your back! I'm a big fan of making things simple, easy, and stress free wherever possible. Here are my secrets to planning a dinner party at the click of your fingers.

Fabulous Food - No Stress!

If cooking isn't your forte or the idea of spending hours in the kitchen doesn't appeal to you, then you'll love these options. The concept of having a chef in your home is becoming more common. There is an abundance of fabulous chefs who will come to your home, prepare, cook and beautifully serve everything for you. The great thing is that you don't have to lift a finger.

Combine this with a done-for-you tablescape that includes everything you need, and creating an epic dinner party becomes magically easy! If you need to keep the costs down, Marks & Spencer or similar stores have lots of ready made foods perfect for dinner parties.

A private chef will take over your kitchen for the evening and consult with you to create the perfect meal for your guests. They will also beautifully serve all the food. You're free to enjoy the evening with your guests and there's no washing up left for you to do!

'*It's so much easier booking a chef to come and do the dinner parties in our house because it then means both me and my husband can spend time with our guests rather than worrying about cooking! We had someone come in and do it for a garden party birthday this year and it was so nice knowing all the decor would be sorted as well as entertainment and food. We got to just relax and enjoy it!*'

— - QUOTE FROM LISA JOHNSON.

Lisa loves hosting parties at home and with a busy schedule, bringing in specialists to support the experience has definitely bought joy to entertaining at home. Lisa hired one of our outdoor dining domes from my event hire business Qube Events.

Creating a Show Stopping Tablescape - No Stress!

The simplest and easiest way to dress your table is to purchase a tablescape. First, let's make it clear, I'm not suggesting for one moment you run around lots of shops trying to find the perfect setting for your dining room table. We're a generation that likes things done for us. Yes, you can buy boxes of beautifully curated decor that will provide you with everything to create an incredible table set up.

I am suggesting that you set the table (unless you want to hire an event designer to come in and style your table), but this is the next best thing. It's rewarding to see your table looking fabulous and knowing that you made it happen (maybe with a little help from your gorgeous tablescape box).

Make sure your tablescape comes with a style guide to show you how to create the perfect look. Often you will find that tablescape companies offer lots of accessories that will compliment the look too, such as cutlery, water jugs, tablecloths etc. Once you've invested in a tablescape, you will use it again and again. (See chapter 12 to find details on how to get your hands on some beautiful tablescapes).

The Dreaded Washing Up - No Stress!

I know many people get put off hosting dinner parties as they know there is so much washing up to do!! Depending on the crowd you're inviting, you might actually enjoy some quality time in the kitchen with a couple of your guests wiping the dishes - and having a great natter at the same time.

When we have massive family gatherings, our solution (for years now) is to bring in someone to help with the washing up. Often if you ask your cleaner, they may be happy to do a few extra hours. They will wash the dishes after each course and keep the kitchen clean and tidy. It's so nice to be able to finish a meal and know that all the washing up is done for you!

Preparing your home for a dinner party

With guests coming over, you want your home to look the part too. Ensure the bathrooms are fully stocked up, along with scented candles or a lovely diffuser. For me, it's making sure the kids' playroom is tidy and I've removed any clutter. My recommendation is to bring a cleaner in before your dinner party. A professional cleaning will make your home feel nice and fresh, ready for your guests' arrival.

Think about what your home looks like from the outside. Do you need a new front door mat? What do guests see as soon as they come through the front door? Lighting some candles around your home always creates a warm inviting atmosphere.

A few simple spruces to your home can make all the difference. You want your guests to feel relaxed, so dim the lights, string up some fairy lights and create a very welcoming atmosphere. Pop on some music, make sure that you have a premade playlist so you don't need to worry about being DJ on the night and just enjoy.

Top tip: a nice apron ensures you don't spoil your gorgeous clothes. Pop it on whilst you are serving to protect your clothes from any splashes.

The success of a dinner party is all in the planning. **"Planning is the beginning of a fabulous evening!!"** says Sharon Brunt-Clarke, my executive assistant.

"Dinner party planning is about making it special. Who are your guests? Is it a night with family or friends, or a dinner party with the Girls (my favourite!!). Choose your theme, think about your menu, how you will dress your table, drinks too - fizz, cocktails, wine, are you dressing for the occasion around a theme (I love a Girls night and ladies in Red!!), making it as special, fun, relaxed, as you can."

Your dinner party checklist, so you can make sure you've ticked all the boxes.

STAGE 1

- Pick a date for your dinner party
- Create your guest list (Make sure you have a big enough table for the number of guests you want to invatation and that you have enough plates, cutlery etc. How many chairs can you fit around your dining room table? You can always buy more, but at least you know).
- Decide on a theme for your dinner, even if it's just a colour theme. This will help so much with the rest of the planning your event. (Look back at Chapter 3 for ideas)
- Decide on a dress code if you're having a theme
- invatation your guests

STAGE 2

- Confirm final numbers and ask for dietary requirements
- Plan your menu & decide on pre-dinner nibbles
- Test any new recipes
- Decide which drinks to offer your guests on arrival
- Pair your wines with your courses
- Write yourself a grocery shopping list
- Stock up your drinks cabinet with drinks you know your guests love

STAGE 3

- Make a list of what needs to be cooked/baked
- Block out some time in your diary for food preparation
- Think about your food dishes and how you are going to serve them. Do you need to buy any new serviceware?
- Check if you have enough glassware for your proposed drinks
- Decide on a theme for dressing your dining room table.
- Tablecloth
- Napkins & Napkin details
- Charger Plates
- Cutlery
- Placemats
- Table runner
- Decor to run down the centre of your table
- Extra touches - Menu Cards, Place Names - you can match your theme.
- Entertainment - Music/Live entertainment - would you like to add some, if so, now is the time to book, or you might create a playlist.
- Dinner party games

STAGE 4

- Rearrange the refrigerator to make space for food
- Decide on your outfit for the dinner party
- Arrange a day to tidy your home before guests arrive/book a cleaner for the day before
- Book a waitress/cleaner to come in and do the washing up during the night
- Think about where you are going to hang guests' coats. Do you need to clear your cloakroom out, so you have space for coats? Or maybe you might want to hire or buy a coat rail.
- Purchase some nice candles, moisturizer and soaps for your bathroom and maybe some candles for your hallway, and of course, make sure you are fully stocked up on toilet paper. It always looks very inviting having candles lit as guests enter.
- Set up your table and enjoy dressing it with beautiful decor (It's always fun to keep this a surprise, especially if other guests in your house are planning on attending).
- Remind your guests what time to be at yours for.

The Day of...

- Buy any extra ice
- Make sure the dishwasher is empty
- Chill wine before guests arrive
- Light candles, arrange fresh flowers if using
- Turn on the music
- Finish any last-minute cooking
- Get ready
- Enjoy!

"THE ULTIMATE
LUXURY IS BEING
ABLE TO RELAX,
PARTY AND ENJOY
YOUR OWN HOME"

DEBBIE MARKS

Chapter Nine

NEXT LEVEL GARDEN PARTIES

*I*n this chapter, I'm going to show you how to plan next level events in your own back garden. This could be a birthday party, wedding, bar/bat mitzvah or special celebration. There is something incredible about hosting events in your own home and I'm going to show you exactly how to do this in a stress free way.

Throughout my career, I have event managed many events in my clients back gardens. Many of them have been hosted in fabulous marquees for weddings, bar/bat mitzvahs and key milestone celebrations. One of my latest events was a fabulous 60th wedding anniversary celebration for a gorgeous couple called Bert and Gloria, who bought their entire family together for a 12-hour long celebration in the grounds of their home, where we planned a black-tie lunch followed by entertainment and a BBQ in the evening. This included several different acts, karaoke (as it was one of Bert's favourite things to do), a DJ and a fireworks show timed to music.

The events that I am going to be talking about in this chapter are predominantly going to be about hosting events in Marquees or temporary structures in your back garden. I use the term temporary structure, because it doesn't have to be a marquee. If you have a big enough garden, you could have a tipi (think Cowboy and Indian style tents) or a stretch tent. If you're hosting small intimate events or a kid's party, you might consider a garden dome/igloo or a bell tent for a fun sleepover (This is on my daughter's wish list for her next birthday).

If you do have large internal spaces in your home then several of the things that we are going to talk about in this chapter may also apply to you.

My first tip for planning a large-scale event at home would actually be to work with an event planner! There are LOTS of moving parts to live events at home and it's really important that you enjoy every minute of your event and not have to worry about any of the logistics. There are lots of elements that go into a next level event at home.

I'm going to touch on these in this chapter so that you understand how much work goes into these. This will particularly help you, if you make the decision to employ a professional to assist you with your planning - you'll know what you're looking for/what they should be doing.

One of the beauties of having an event at home where you're putting up a large structure in your back garden means that you can make the most of it the entire weekend/a few days, so you may wish to use it for multiple purposes. An example of this is where I have had several clients who have used marquees for their son or daughters bar or bat mitzvah and have used the marquee for a Friday night dinner, lunch and then a party in the evening on Sunday night. The marquee was sectioned into smaller areas to accommodate smaller guest numbers and then opened up to everyone for the Sunday night. Some of them have kept it up even longer and hosted a charity event following their private event.

Firstly, let's start off with **why you might decide to host an event at home instead of hiring a venue** for your special occasion. I always get asked the question, is it cheaper to host an event at home instead of hiring a venue?

The simple answer to this is, if you are going to keep the event at home very low key, then you may be able to bring it in cheaper than some venues, however, it will all depend on the area that you live in and where you would like to host the event. On the whole, having a temporary structure at home can often work out a more costly experience than a venue, as you are basically building your events facility and structure from scratch and you need to bring in everything for it. The beauty of this is that you have a complete blank canvas to work from and as I said earlier, there is something really special about inviting your guests into your own home. Also, all the memories you are going to create at your event will be at your home and that's so special. If my garden was big enough, I would 100% be having big celebrations in my own garden over a venue any day.

The Entrance

I have planned several events where the entrance to the event is in through the front door of the house and it then takes guests through your house and out to a beautiful marquee in the back garden. Some people choose to keep guests completely out of the house and use a side entrance instead keeping the event contained to its own structure and keeping everyone out of the house.

Before we start let's talk about some of the practicalities of hosting an event at home. The space. The last thing I want you to do is put lots of plans in place and then find out that it's not feasible to do what you are hoping to do.

A few key elements to think about before you 100% confirm your event at home.

1) How much space do you have for a temporary structure?

Are there lots of trees in your garden that will make the space tricky to work with? It is really important to know your numbers and how many guests that you are trying to get into the space. If you contact a marquee company they should come and do a site visit to your home; they will measure up to see what's feasible and will be able to advise how many guests will fit. You will need to have an initial idea of the layout you are looking for, too.

2) Are there any restrictions in the area in terms of loud music on the night?

I would inform your neighbours that you are planning on having an event and either invatation them or suggest they go away for the weekend or pay for them to go away for the night so that you don't get complaints from your neighbours. Think about the houses that are either side of your house but also think if there are any houses behind yours too. The last thing you want on the night is for one of your neighbours to be complaining about the noise and calling the police - your party could potentially close down or they could ask you to turn the music right down, which might spoil the atmosphere. I am telling you all of this from experience because I have had neighbours at the front door of my clients' houses where I have had to mitigate and try and calm them down because they couldn't get their baby to sleep due to the loud music.

3) Parking

Where would guests park? Are there certain areas around or is it better to advise all of your guests to come in taxis?

4) Toilets

Do you have enough for the number of guests attending? If not, consider hiring luxury portable toilets.

5) Catering

Do you have enough space for the caterers to work from? Your kitchen often won't suffice as they will have large ovens to bring in. If you have a garage, your caterer could set up a kitchen in there, or if you're having a marquee and your garden is large enough, I would recommend adding on a catering marquee.

6) Power

I wouldn't recommend running the power for a large event from your house, I have seen too many fuse switches blow. I'd highly recommend hiring a generator, along with a technician to sort out all the power distribution. (Do you see now why an event planner is a good idea?)

7) Lighting

How are you going to light up your space? Ensure that driveways are lit so that as guests are leaving, they can find their way out. It also makes for a dramatic entrance. I'd always recommend bringing in a big lighting rig to really make a marquee spectacular, but you might op for more decorative lighting such as festoons or fairy lights, or why not have a mix of both?

Throughout this chapter, I am going to tell you a couple of stories of my favourite all-time parties at home. I've done a lot and they've been pretty fun. I'm hoping that by telling you some of these stories you can take some inspiration for your own events and put your own stamp on them to create something spectacular.

Deborah's 40th Birthday Party

If you want to celebrate a 40th birthday in style, how this beautiful lady celebrated was pretty epic. The inspiration of the party came because the family had planned to go to Lio's, which is a prestigious cabaret club in Ibiza. However, due to the pandemic they couldn't get all of their guests out there. This was one of Debbie's most favourite places that she had ever been to, so her husband decided to throw her a party at home that was to basically replicate the club in Ibiza.

We looked at various space options in their very large home. We chose to hold the event in the basement of the house, where they had a swimming pool, gym and cinema room. They did consider a marquee in their garden too. The preference was to have the event inside, so that's what we made happen. The first challenge was to cover their pool as we needed more floor space. We bought in a specialist company to cover over the swimming pool to create a large space for the event. The basement of the house had different rooms. We turned one room into the bar with a wall-to-wall shimmer wall, one into a casino games room, and the other room was where the stage, live music dancing, entertainment and chill out furniture was located.

We wanted to create a full experience for these clients so we sent out an invitation in the same colour schemes and we created a bespoke logo for the party that was similar to the logo of the nightclub.

As guests arrived on the night, there was a long driveway which we lined with a 50m long dramatic red carpet. As guests entered the driveway, they were met with fire performers roaming throughout the garden and stilt walking showgirls in beautiful, dramatic, white feather costumes.

The entire house and gardens were illuminated in red and the entranceway of the house was dressed in beautiful dramatic florals. As guests came into the house, they were greeted by showgirls and had their photos at a banner with the client's logo on, just like you see at the at the BAFTAs.

The hallway was lit with lanterns and candles, and guests were welcomed with cocktails and bubbly on arrival. We had a saxophone player roaming the space, along with an excellent magician to keep guests entertained.

Once all the guests had arrived, we made an official start to the entertainment of the night and all of the performers for the night made a grand entrance from outside down a dramatic staircase with fire and indoor pyros, all choreographed to welcome in a fabulous international burlesque performer who had an incredible voice and acted as a compere for the evening. She interacted with Debra and the family and sang some spectacular songs. This was a real showpiece and definitely brought the audience together. I watched the film back recently for this event and the smiles and laughter on everyone's faces was amazing to see.

We built a custom stage in the sunken garden and had a dedicated mobile bar. We covered the carpet in the client's cinema room with our own carpet so it didn't damage the floor. In the main space, we bought in a sparkly dancefloor. The pool area had glass panels on the floor so you could see through and see the swimming pool underneath. On this area we also created a multi-tiered catwalk, finished in red glitter, that dancers used to perform on. We had seating going all around this as we wanted to have the guests as interactive as possible with everything going on. The DJ sat on a custom-built area on top of the Jacuzzi, with a branded red glitter DJ booth with the client's logo on front. Oh, and we had a snake charmer too, which was a huge hit with guests!

Sylvie's Batmitzvah

Theme: Festival Garden Party

Guests: Kids, Adult Friends & Family

Colour Scheme: Hot pink, orange, yellow & green

Sylvie's party was so vibrant and colourful, I absolutely loved it. Our client has a large garden so we filled this with a beautifully lined marquee, which was swagged with colourful fabric bunting and festoon lights which also lined the driveway. The party had a very earthy vibe to it, with bare wooden tables, chairs, benches and wooden barrel poseur tables. Some tables were covered with a stone-coloured tablecloth and the tables were laced with vintage crystal vases of the most beautiful, brightly coloured, fresh flowers. We created a bespoke wooden panel style bar for the event, with half barrel troughs on top which were filled with bottles of beers, along with two food stations to match, which the catered had filled with a magnificent array of brightly coloured salads, meat assortments and delicacies.

Outside the marquee, we had an ice cream bike with parasol and a campervan photo booth which we had styled with Sylvie's name in bright coloured glitter letters with lights on top of it. There was a glitter artist and cute touches like chalkboard signs that said 'Jazz up your Gin' next to a dedicated Gin bar. I always know an event is a success as I get lots of phone calls the next day from different people wanting similar for their parties! Let's say we got lots of phone calls the next day.

"THE MORE YOU
PRAISE AND
CELEBRATE YOUR
LIFE, THE MORE
THERE IS IN LIFE
TO CELEBRATE."

OPRAH WINFREY

Chapter Ten

EXTRAORDINARY MILESTONE EVENTS

*M*ilestone celebrations are what life is all about! These are the moments when we bring our loved ones together and create beautiful memories that will last a lifetime.

One thing I have learnt in life is that ***we are responsible*** *for making the moments that become our memories.* By choosing to fully celebrate the special times, we are creating a life for ourselves full of richness and enjoyment.

Planning these celebrations can be rewarding and often, it's as much fun as the celebration itself. Nobody is going to throw these parties for us. So, it's on us to step up and say, this is important to me and I'm going to have fun with it.

This chapter is all about life-cycle events. We have an opportunity here to honour the stages that make up our cycle of life. It's important to treasure these milestone events, as a way of showing our loved ones how important they are to us.

This chapter will cover the following milestone and life cycle events.

Baby Events

- Gender Reveals
- Baby Showers

Kids Parties

Wedding Events

- Proposals
- Engagement Parties
- Hen/Bachelorette Parties
- The Wedding
- Wedding Anniversaries

Milestone Birthdays

- Sweet 16
- 18th Birthday
- 21st Birthday
- Decade Parties

Graduations

Celebration of Achievement Parties

New Home / House Warming

Many of the principles and elements discussed in previous chapters can also be applied to the celebrations below.

Here you will find a selection of party themes, ideas and activities. Feel free to dip in and out of this section every time you have a special celebration to plan.

BABY EVENTS

These events are all about the joy and excitement of bringing a baby into the world! That's certainly something to be celebrated. Becoming a parent, especially for the first time, is a huge deal. Whether you're planning baby events for yourself, a friend, or a family member, have fun with it.

Gender Reveals

As soon as that baby bump is visible, friends and loved ones are eager to know whether it's going to be a girl or a boy. A gender reveal party is a fun and memorable way to celebrate the surprise and anticipation of a son or daughter. This is a growing trend where creativity can run wild.

If you're involved in planning your own baby's gender reveal, you can also be surprised. Ask your doctor to place the gender information in a sealed envelope that you can give to whoever is helping you plan.

You might want to keep this as an intimate celebration, with only immediate family in attendance, or create a large-scale party for all your friends and relatives. Whichever you choose, here are some ideas to do the big reveal in style:

Gender reveal piñata: have a fun-shaped piñata filled with pink or blue wrapped candies, then hit it with a stick until you have the answer. Ole!

Pop Surprise: poke a giant balloon to reveal lots of mini pink or blue balloons inside

Colour explosion: gender reveal smoke bombs/powder cannons/confetti cannons (these make great photos)

The oversized present: Open the lid of a giant gift-wrapped box to discover which colour of helium balloons go flying up into the air.

Bun in the Oven party: Every guest receives a cupcake with a blue or pink filling hidden in the centre. The gender is revealed as people bite into their desserts.

Gender reveal chocolate bomb or cake smash: crack into them and reveal the colour of the sweets in the centre.

Harry Potter Gender reveal: Fun for wizarding parents - let the *sorting hat* reveal the gender. Gather your friends around the hat and lift up to reveal a pink or blue item of baby clothing. Magical food and decor round out the Hogwarts theme.

Open up: Stuff an umbrella with coloured confetti and open it over the parents-to-be.

Fountain of Colour: Set up a white chocolate fountain, then present the parents-to-be with food dye in a concealed bottle. Mum and Dad will pour the dye into the top and delight the guests as the fountain turns pink or blue.

Sports themed gender reveal - ask your guests to wear shirts to show if they're rooting for team pink or blue. Pitch a powder-filled ball (baseball, football, tennis, etc.) to the proud parents. When they hit the ball, the colourful results will get cheers!

Baby Showers

You probably are familiar with these parties. It's when you gather to "shower" the mum-to-be with lots of gorgeous gifts for her and the baby (usually before the little one arrives). Guests turn up to the baby shower with adorable gifts in hand. Cute baby clothes and accessories are decked out in sweet, baby-themed wrappings.

These events are often held one or two months before the baby's due date. Speaking from experience, be sure you don't leave it too late! I planned a last-minute baby shower for my cousin, Samantha. When her baby, Lily, decided to make an early arrival, we ended up hosting a post-birth baby shower instead!

A baby shower is usually thrown by friends or family members. Guests bring gifts and cards. There are fun foods to eat, baby games to play, and fabulous photo opportunities with the mummy-to-be. Many baby showers are held at home, but they don't have to be. You could hire a venue.

Celebrities have been known to throw some very extravagant baby showers! Khloe Kardashian had an elaborate elephant-themed baby shower at the Hotel Bel-Air in Los Angeles. It involved a pink flower wall, floral covered ceiling, giant elephant topiary, and hundreds of balloons. Khloe had all her guests dressed in pink and there was a custom-made neon sign spelling out "Baby Thompson."

Baby Shower Theme Ideas

Having a baby shower theme is a great opportunity to unleash your creativity and it will help a lot of the plans slot into place nicely.

A few cute theme ideas to consider:

Elephants
Oh Boy!
Oh Baby!
Nautical
Dinosaurs
Little Pumpkin (Great for an autumn/fall shower)
Pretty in Paris
Mother to Bee/ Little Honey Bee / Everyone is buzzing about the baby and Mummy-to-be (We're adding to our hive)
Astronauts
Rubber Ducks
Wonder Woman
Butterflies
Bunnies
Enchanted Garden

Mermaids
Lady-Birds
Safari
Sunflowers
Friends
Winter/Frozen
Twinkle Twinkle Little Star
Unicorns "A Magical Day is on its way"
Winnie The Pooh
Princess
Le Petit Prince
Teddy Bear
Rainbow Baby
Peter Pan in Neverland
Baby in Bloom (Lots of florals!)
The Adventure Begins
Ready to Pop
Noah's Ark
Botanical Baby/Baby Succulent
Cowboy "A little Cowboy is coming to town!"
Boho Baby Shower (Ideal for a free-spirited mummy)
Afternoon Tea "A baby girl/boy is brewing"
Woodland animal theme - foxes, deers, owls & other furry friends.

Baby Shower Decoration Ideas

I'd always recommend matching your decorations to your theme. Here are some ideas that you can tailor to suit your taste.

Welcome sign
Balloon garlands
Backdrops e.g., Flower walls, sequin walls (lots of variations available)
Dream catchers
Flower crowns

Flower garlands
Table scatter
Star garlands
Cute baby banners/bunting
Use quirky containers to serve food from
Giant Baby blocks
Cute cupcake cases & toppers
Paper lanterns

Tableware to match your theme, for more elegant baby showers use glass charger plates and coloured glassware

Baby Shower Game Ideas

- Baby Bingo
- Mummy or Daddy (give mummy and daddy to be paddles that say mummy or daddy on each side. Ask the couple questions and let's see what answers are given and if mummy & daddy agree!) e.g.,, Who will more likely be the parent that says no? Who's going to get up most in the middle of the night?
- Name that baby tune - This one is pretty much what it says on the tin. Play snippets of baby songs and let your guests guess what the song is. Whoever guesses the most is the winner.
- Diaper Challenge. Blindfold mummy & daddy. Give them a doll each and a nappy (diaper) and let's see who can put the nappy on the quickest.
- Who knows mummy best? - Read out a list of questions about mummy and get your guests to answers, whoever gets the most right is the winner.
- Baby Photos - ask your guests to bring pics of themselves as a baby, mix them all up and let your guests guess who's who.
- My water broke! - for this you need some tiny plastic

baby dolls, put them into an ice cube tray, fill with water, and freeze. Give each guest an ice cube and then the race is on as each person tries to find the best way possible to get baby out. Whoever does it the quickest wins and shouts "My water broke!"

- Guess the baby food - Your adventurous guests taste a spoonful of baby food and guess the flavour! This can be done blindfolded for extra fun.

- Pass the Parcel - Inside each layer of the parcel is a baby gift & a piece of advice for mummy-to-be.

- Place the dummy (pacifier) in the baby's mouth - the same concept as *pin the tail on the donkey* in baby shower style. Hang up a giant picture of a baby, each guest gets a cardboard picture of dummy with her name on it (and some tack on the back), and takes a turn to wear a blind fold and "give baby the dummy." Whoever gets closest to the baby's mouth is the winner.

- Do you know your Disney Babies? Quiz your guests on the names of Disney character babies. Or match the mum to the baby (e.g., Simba next to Sarabi). Whoever gets the most correct wins.

- Don't Say Baby! - As each guest arrives, give them a safety pin to put onto their clothes. If they say the word baby when talking to someone, the person they are talking to steals their pin. Whoever gets the most pins at the end of the event wins.

- The Price is Right - We all know having a baby is expensive! Play to see who can guess the actual cost of baby supplies. The winner is whoever comes the closest to the real price.

- How well do you know your nursery rhymes? - Sing the first line of a nursery rhyme, who can guess the rest of the verse? Or have a line of a nursery rhyme, leave out the blanks and let your guests fill them in.

- Baby bucket list - get your guests to write a list of must-do things they should do with their baby in its first year.
- Bottle Race! This is a great game if you have men at the baby shower. Have a load of baby bottles and fill them with a beverage, whoever drinks as fast as possible and finishes the bottle first is the winner!
- Baby Shower A-Z - each guest has a piece of paper and pen and writes the full alphabet down one side. Guests have to come up with a baby related word for each letter of the alphabet. Whoever gets the most in one minute is the winner (e.g., for B - Bottle, C - Crib)
- Baby Songs! - Get your guests to write a list of songs down that include the word baby, whoever gets the most wins.
- Guess the size of the bump! - You'll need a tape measure for this, everyone guesses how big the bump is, the closest size wins.
- Baby name ideas - Have a chalk board for guests to give you name ideas.

Message ideas to write in baby shower cards

- I can't wait to meet your baby.
- Your little family is about to get bigger & cuter.
- I'm so happy for you.
- Wishing both you and your new baby all the best.
- Wishing you moments of joy with your new little baby.
- Can't wait to meet the latest addition to your family.
- Thanks in advance for naming the baby after me!
- I can't wait to see who the baby resembles more.
- Say hello to your bundle of joy and goodbye to sleeping in ever again!
- Congratulations on your baby's arrival! I know you'll be a terrific mum.
- From one mother to another, the moment you set eyes on

your little one, you'll be smitten forever.

KIDS BIRTHDAYS

Our kids grow up so fast! Blink and they will be at university. Birthday parties give us a chance to celebrate each child and help them feel special. Plus, your birthday boy or girl has a whole heap of fun whilst creating memories they can look back on years from now.

It doesn't need to be just fun for the kids, it can be a whole load of fun for the adults too. I know now when I look back at my kids' parties, the ones I 100% put the most effort in for were the best parties and ones that people still talk about today. You might think the thought of a kid's party would drive you insane, or you might love all the planning. Either way, if you follow the principles we've learnt earlier in the book and give yourself plenty of time in advance, you can have such a fun experience planning a kid's party. For me, watching the pure joy and excitement on my kids faces is what it's all about and when my kids turn round and say that was the best birthday ever! This is when you know it was all worth it.

Below you will find a list of themes/ ideas for kid's parties. You can vary the theme and activities to suit the age range. Remember, it's often the little details that will take your party from ordinary to extraordinary, so make time for the little touches.

Theme Ideas

One in a Melon (1st birthday)
Winter Wonderland
Snow Princess
Enchanted Fairies
Flamingo Party
Mermaid Party

Under the Sea
Pirates, Princesses & Heroes
Treasure Island
Carousel Party
Dragons, Knights & Damsels
Wacky Science
Dinosaur
Unicorn
Glow party
Jungle safari
Spooktacular Monsters
Pop star party
All star sports party
Beach Party
Teddy Bears Picnic (Ask kids to bring their favourite teddy
bear/stuffed animal)
Farmyard Party e.g., Farmer 'Jack's' Party
Carnival theme
Elf on the Shelf
Hot tub party
Movie night (mini boxes of popcorn are a must for this)
Circus party
Rainbow theme
Lego theme
Firefighter
Cowboy & Cowgirls
Gingerbread house tea party
Under the Sea
Nautical Party
Pirate Party
Digger party
I'm in the Army now
Tik Tok party
Space Party/Galaxy Party
Game On

Grand Prix

Character Party

Minions Party
Moana Party
Peter Rabbit Party
Frozen Party
Batman/Superman/Marvel Party
Sesame Street
Minnie/Mickey Disney Party
Star Wars
Curious George - Lets Go Bananas!
Pokémon party
Finding Dory
Emoji Party
Peppa Pig
Sponge Bob
Harry Potter
Trolls
Toy Story
Baby Shark
Tellytubbies
Super Mario Brothers
Fortnite
PJ Masks

Activity Ideas

Slumber party
Science party
Disco Party (Glow Disco, Laser Disco)
Football party
Magic, Disco & Games party
Parachute

Craft party
Cooking party
Treasure hunt
Piñata
Ice cream bar
Puppet show (Loved by kids 5 and under)
Traditional Party Games (Pin the tail, duck duck goose, pass the parcel, musical statues etc.)
Muddy run
Mobile zoo party
Bugs party
Balloon artist
Chocolate making
Camping party
Pamper party (Could include bath bomb making)
Swimming/pool party
Karaoke party
Drama party
Arty Party
Paint Party
Soft play
Gymnastics
Trampolining
Roller-skate/Ice Skating party
Bouncy castle/Inflatables
Its a knockout party
Pizza making party
Dance party
Slime making party
Story telling party

Here are some of my top tips when it comes to planning your kid's party. These are all relevant whatever your budget is. I've also included a few budget tips at the end, as well as some examples of some luxury, crazy, extraordinary parties!

- Get the birthday girl/boy involved with choosing the theme, run some ideas by them and go with the one they get most excited about. It's always good to do a little research first and propose themes that you know are achievable and then give them a choice of a few themes to choose from.
- Create a Pinterest board of party theme ideas to gather your ideas and then choose your favourites.
- Design invatations to match the theme.
- If you are having a theme, get the kids to dress up.
- When you theme, you theme! So, think about everything you are doing, how could you incorporate it into the theme? E.g., from the moment guests enter, you could have a sign outside, themed food, invatation, entertainers, giant props for kids to have photos with etc.
- Theme your going home gifts.
- If you are having adults stay at your party, make sure you have some food and drink for them to enjoy. The more relaxed they are, you will be too. Create a simple food and drink station where adults can help themselves.
- If you're having a joint party, make sure your ideas are compatible. Don't match yourself with a penny pincher if you're a party spender or vice versa. Have a quick coffee if you don't know the other person well, to see if your ideas and values align.
- End a kid's party with bubbles! Investing in a bubble blowing machine is a great idea and you'll find yourself bringing it out year on year!
- Get extra help! Can you rope in the grandparents, aunties or uncles to help out? If you are doing everything yourself, who can you use to help you set everything up/prep the food etc.? They can help you with putting up the decorations, preparing food, taking coats, running games, loo trips, cutting the birthday cake for party bags

and clearing up. Make sure you give clear tasks to everyone helping.

- For a hassle-free party, hire an entertainer/party planning company. If you are looking for an extraordinary high-end kid's party, there are lots of specialist event planning companies that can help you with. Many kid's party companies will take care of everything for you, from the entertainment, invatations, decorations and more.

- When it comes to choosing the day, after school parties mean you still get to keep your weekend free or doing just family birthday related celebrations. Saturday parties give you more time to recover and Sunday parties give you more time to prepare.

- Two hours is a really good amount of time for a kid's party, whatever their age. It gives you time for some activities, food and time to sing happy birthday with the cake.

- If you want to save the birthday cake for family/adults, give the kids cupcakes as going home presents.

- Popular party venues get booked early, so even if you don't plan anything else yet, think ahead and secure your date. This also goes to say with really good party entertainers.

- As soon as you know the date of your party, share it with your kid's parents. E.g., if you have a WhatsApp or parents Facebook group, share it in there. Once you have all the details confirmed, you can then follow up with an invitation.

- This seems like an obvious one... But just in case, whether you are at a venue or at home, remove anything that could be breakable, or have sharp edges that might cause an accident. Remember, it's quite likely once the kids have some sugar inside them, they will be running around! If you are having a party at home, only leave out toys you know they are happy for other children to play with too.

- When it comes to drinks and spillages, a closed cup works a treat. Choose something like a drinks carton or you could go with something more fun like a plastic disco ball and straw, filled with juice. These always go down a treat. My kids love them too and I'm often bringing them out now when we have kids round to our house to play.
- One of my favourite easiest and mess free ways of serving foods is to give all the kids their very own party box of food. They can be disposed of easy; all the rubbish can go back in their boxes and they look super cute too... and you can also tie them into your theme. The food can be still be fun and presented in a stylish way in your boxes.
- Another easy solution for parties, with little prep, is to serve up pizzas.

Tips if you are planning on a budget

- Timing is key. Plan your party from 2pm - 5pm, guests won't expect a full meal.
- Share the party with a friend. If your child has a birthday party close to one of their friends, plan together and split the costs.
- Go digital for the invatations.
- Pick up party favours in the sales - start early and stock up as the sales come out.
- Choose crafts that double up as favours.

I couldn't let this chapter go by without sharing with you some of the fabulous and, some of us might call crazy, I like to call them 'extraordinary 'party ideas that some well-known celebrities have done for their kid's parties. All these things are possible and I always say, if you've got the money, then there is nothing more special than using it to create memories through parties for your friends and family. Enjoy these.

Jessica Simpson hired dancers and performers for her son's Moana themed party. Each guest took home personalised pineapple printed goody bags filled with toys. Jessica transformed her back garden into the Isle of Te Fiti, where the film was based, and had dancers and performers dressed to look like the characters.

The Kardashian family transformed their garden into a festival for North's first birthday. This included a ferris wheel, karaoke stage, tipi tents and bouncy castles. They named the party 'Kid-chella' after the famous Cochella festival.

Beyoncé and Jay-Z's Blue Ivy had a mega princess party. The venue was decorated with flowers from the ceiling and children's teepees. There were fairy characters roaming everywhere and each guest could dress up in a princess costume with fairy wings provided by the hosts. There was even archery and a makeup station!

MILESTONE BIRTHDAYS

Birthday celebrations are a big deal, no matter how old you are. I feel they are really important as it makes us feel really special and it's also an opportunity for you to make someone else feel really special. It's an opportunity for people around you to show how much they love you too. Many of us lead busy lives and our mindset can be really affected or we can get bogged down with things, but when we know we have a birthday coming up, it's something to look forward to, something to get excited about, so I believe that just by celebrating a birthday, that' a pick me up in itself.

Birthdays are also great ways for making relationships and family bonds stronger. Just think how many parties or celebrations you've been to over the years where you may have networked, had really meaningful conversations, maybe even met your partner or just laughed, relaxed and released energy and let your hair down. Ok... so have I convinced you enough yet to throw a party?

I celebrated my 21st recently... ok, I mean my 40th and my family arranged a really special birthday celebration for me. We bought our closest family together in a little chalet where we stayed and celebrated for the weekend. If it wasn't for a birthday, I can't have guaranteed that this weekend would have happened, so I have me turning 40 to thank and actually, it's really not that bad turning 40. In fact, it's pretty awesome.

In this section, you'll find some age specific ideas that will help you celebrate your milestone birthday in an extraordinary way! Let's start with the Sweet 16.

SWEET 16

A Sweet 16 party is a coming-of-age party for a young girl and traditionally has been their first formal party. The Sweet 16 tradition trend started in the United States and it celebrates approaching adulthood. Some girls will consider the 16th birthday as one of the most important birthday celebrations of their lives. In the US, it's when girls learn to drive, can get jobs and take on other adult responsibilities. The highlight of the sweet 16 is of course, the party! Often, this is a party a little girl will dream of for years and they are often very specific about what they want and what they don't want!

There are lots of theories of the origin of the Sweet 16. Many link the party to the Mexican Quinceanera, which takes place on the girl's 16th birthday, or to the Mediterranean European coming of age celebrations, which were held when a woman was presented to court the first time as eligible for marriage.

There are a few traditions that take place at a Sweet 16 party which I wanted to share with you. Also, please note that because the Sweet 16 party is huge in the United States, there is no reason why you can't adopt this tradition in the rest of the world or, if you're just interested to learn what it's all about, here's some insights!

1. **Shoe and Crowning Ceremony** - The girl of honour walks with her date wearing a pair of slippers or flat shoes or, more commonly today, trainers (or sneakers, for the Americans reading this). The tiara and the shoes are bought out by her father or other significant male in her family. Whilst she sits in a chair, her father takes off her slippers and puts on her new shoes (usually a fabulous pair of heels). After putting on the shoes, the father puts her tiara on to crown her head. This is supposed to represent a symbol of her transition into womanhood. Sometimes the mother will be responsible for placing the tiara.

2. **Candle Lighting Ceremony** - Lighting of 16 candles acknowledges those closest to the 16-year-old such as parents, siblings, grandparents, cousins, friends etc. Each get to say a little message for the celebrant and light a candle for them.

3. **Father and daughter dance** - This happens right at the beginning of the partying! The father and daughter share a dance together. First of all, the father will present the daughter to all their guests and often give a mushy speech talking about how proud he is and some of the special moments they have had together over the years. They will then dance to a slow song that is special to them both.

For those looking for something a bit more low key, an outdoor movie night is always fun.

Below, you'll find lots of ideas for milestone parties. Yes, of course you can mix and match between the age groups, it will depend on how young at heart you and your guests are!

18th Birthday

Here's a few fun party ideas for an 18th.

- **Create your own nightclub** A blacked out marquee in the garden would be fabulous for this, or transforming a space in your home if it's large enough. You could hire a venue or even exclusively hiring a nightclub or fancy restaurant will do the trick for this. I've worked in lots of bland event spaces and we've completely transformed them to look like nightclubs. Make sure you have a super cool DJ too.

- **Host a drive in Movie Night** - This is really fun! Rent a giant movie screen, a projector and show the birthday person's favourite film. Serve popcorn and drinks to your guests through the car windows. If you don't have the space to do it, often a local public park will let you rent out some space for a nominal fee.

- **Sleepover Party!** Sleepovers are a bit different when you're 18, but often filled with horror films/romcom, fun sleepover games and lots of junk food. There is no reason why you can't go extraordinary with your sleepover with fun little touches you've learnt about earlier on. There's no reason why you couldn't have a photo booth at home for the night, you can have a lot of fun with friends capturing really special moments.

- **Retro Roller-Skating Party** - Do you even remember the last time you went roller skating? Just imagine taking over your local rink, disco lights on, ask your guests to dress in fabulous retro outfits and enjoy the fun! Play games on the rink, eat hot dogs and drink slushy's and have an incredible time.

- **Sugar High** - Dessert Party. If your teenager has a super sweet tooth, they are going to love this style of party. Ask your guests to bring their favourite desserts, cakes, biscuits, sweet selection. You could also hire in lots of fun sweet desserts such as a Pan Ice machine, Waffle stand and a PicnMix station.

21st Birthdays

- **Fancy dress parties** - These parties are so much fun. We had a family fancy dress party for my brother Ashley's 21st and I will never forget it. Guests were asked to come dressed as characters from films, especially kids' films if I remember. You'll always remember the guests that go above and beyond with their costumes in years to come. I remember my grandma Audrey, she dressed up as Harry Potty! She had glasses just like Harry and walked in with a Potty in her hand. I remember her being in fits of laughter when entering our home, she properly got the giggles, it was hilarious and I'll always remember that moment. My dad dressed head to toe as Shrek, my brother as Noddy and my husband and I dressed up as the Looney Tunes characters Tweety Pie & Sylvester. I just remember my husband chasing me round the house, trying to be in character!

- **Paintball party** - This is a fabulous group activity. Choose a location near to where you live or if you are booking a weekend away for your birthday, somewhere local to where you are staying. The more the merrier when it comes to paintball, you'll find out who will become the hero or villain of the day. It's always fun to dress up the birthday person in a fancy outfit. You put your guests in teams and the winning team will go away with a bottle of bubbly.

- **Murder mystery parties** - To go extraordinary lengths with a murder mystery party, hire a spooky looking venue/accommodation and host a dinner party, where you ask all your guests to dress up. You can also hire in actors to lead the murder mystery, dress up the venue with interactive crime scenes and watch the investigation unfold throughout the night.
- **Karaoke party** - Either book out a private karaoke room or bring the karaoke to your own home and watch your guests sing their hearts out. Ensure your pals play back up dancers and make sure you remember to sing a wild "Happy Birthday" whilst you bring out the cake.
- **Paint and Sip Party** - An adult painting party is super fun. Canvasses, easels a paint palette, painting tutor and glass of champagne! See what crazy creations you and your friends come up with.
- **Boozy Brunch** - For this one you could go out to a lovely boujee restaurant or you could host this at home. It's pretty much what it says in the title. Lots of bubbles and plenty of food and great conversation with good friends.
- **Mixology Party** - You could do this one at home or in a bar. You and your guests will learn how to create the most stylish cocktail, shake them up 'Tom Cruise stylee' and enjoy.
- **Pool Party** - I've seen some fabulous pool parties and you can have a lot of fun with them. Whether you live in a tropical country or you have a covered pool in your home, go to town with it. Make sure you have a photo area to have some fun photos with your friends, a sequin style wall always works well, lots of crazy inflatables too. Drinking games, DJ & BBQ are a great trio.
- **Luxurious Picnic** - This is a lovely idea for a summer birthday celebration. Find a beautiful spot outdoors, either in a garden, park or lovely woodland and set up

some wooden pallets to create your tables. Have coloured cushions around the edges for your guests to sit on, with some decor down the centre, such as vases of fresh flowers and some scented candles to keep any midges away. Take a beautiful picnic hamper of goodies, lay the table with gorgeous plates and coloured glassware and enjoy.

30th Birthdays

Here's some extraordinary ideas for celebrating a 30th birthday.

Rave in a Cave

Yes, you read that right, in a cave! There are some spectacular caves around the world you can hire for a party. Creative lighting inside a cave looks spectacular. Here's a few caves that are famous for their raves/event spaces to give you some inspiration.

- Punta Cana Nightclub, Dominican Republic
- Grotto Bay Beach Resort & Spa, Bermuda
- Hell Fire Caves, England
- Chislehurst Caves, England
- The Caves, Edinburgh, Scotland
- Cabaret Cave, Perth, Australia

40th Birthdays

40 is a great age to throw a really special birthday party. Usually between 20-40 there are a lot of life changes that take place, marriage, kids, jobs, new home etc. Your 40s are prime years and often the start of the best part of your life! Whether you are planning a massive party or an intimate celebration, the same creativity and passion can go into it to enable it to be an extraordinary celebration.

You will see earlier, I talked about my client Deborah's epic 40th Lio themed party. Now this was one hell of a party and definitely an incredible way to start your 40s. A night filled with magnificent live entertainment, a snake performer, indoor pyros, outdoor fire performers, quirky cocktails and a full transformation of the basement of their home, where they have their pool, into a nightclub. We even ensured that Deborah had a 3 tiered cake to match the theme which had a ice fountain (a fancy sparkler) on top. When all the guests sang Happy Birthday, all the bar staff came out with bottles and fountains of flames coming out the bottles.

Here's a few 40th birthday ideas that you could incorporate into a 40th birthday celebration.

40 messages from 40 friends - this is a really thoughtful idea. If you're having a party, you could get all the friends to pre record a short video and show it on a big screen as a surprise on the night.

40th Birthday (1980s) Party. - Ask your friends to dress up in all the gear and play hits from the year you were born. Think Blondie, Queen and Kool and the Gang,

Get everyone involved! - Including the bar staff, waiting staff at your event. Get all the staff wearing branded t-shirts that say any of the following.

- Damn, you make 40 look good!
- Forty & Foxy
- Forty & Fine!
- Congrats on turning 20 for the second time
- Let's drink some Red, Red Wine, Cause UB40 now. (Apologies for this one, I know, I know, it's very cringe! But for any UB40 fans out there, this one if for you!)

50th, 60th, 70th Birthday Party

I have a favourite memory of my dad's 50th birthday party when I was 17. My dad threw an 'Allo 'Allo!' party. For those of you who don't know what this is, it's a British sitcom television series which focuses on the life of a cafe owner 'René', who shows some similarities to my dad (well, the moustache he had at the time), set in the French town of Nouvion during the German occupation of France, in the second World War.

It's very funny and one of dad's favourite TV programmes of the time. My mum decked out our conservatory to look like a French cafe. We had lots of tables with red and white checkered tablecloths, empty wine bottles on the tables with candles in them with drippings all coming down the side, and French bunting around the windows. My parents lived in Paris when they were first married, so the French theme meant a lot to them. Guests were served crepes, which my brother made. I remember dressing up as a waitress all in black with a white frilly apron, and I was there helping to serve the food.

Here's some **extraordinary ways you can celebrate your 50th**.

Charter a boat/yacht

Sure, this sounds a bit extravagant, but you'd be set for a surely memorable birthday. Just think, you and a few close friends and family, popping the cork of a bottle, celebrating your special day. On board, throw a dinner party and end the day watching the sun go down from the coastline. A pure magical day.

Throw a surprise party

So, this one is a tip off for your friends and family, or you might be reading this thinking "what can I do for someone special?". A few tips to make sure the birthday person doesn't find out: Create a code name for the party! Create a whats app group to put all the plans in place and please make sure everyone involved, including all their family, knows it's a surprise. If you're planning a surprise party, make sure you know your birthday person really well and be sensitive to what they would really like, not what you think they would like! E.g., don't go planning a karaoke party because you think it will help their confidence, but secretly you know that the thought of going near a microphone terrifies them.

Themed Dinner Parties

Start with the invatations, through to the dressing of the table, the entertainment, music and the food. Choose a theme and go all out. Check out the dinner party and theming chapters earlier in the book.

Dinner Party in a Fabulous Location

Take your guests for dinner in a location they would never usually go to, or find an exclusive location that's not easily accessible to the general public. One of my favourite dinner locations of all time has to be in Geneva, at the top of a mountain. We took a cable car with our group to the top of the mountain to see spectacular views, where we dined around large wooden tables with benches and a sharing fondue menu. The most magnificent Swiss cheeses and fine wines. This was years ago and I still remember it like it was yesterday.

Dinner in the Sky - this is available in various locations around the world.

If you're not one for heights you might want to avoid this one. Diners are strapped to a table which is on a crane and you are all elevated around 30m (100ft) in the air. Many locations have guest chefs, devising really special menus. Not one for the faint hearted!

A 60th birthday is a big deal, a celebration you are going to want to make really special. Why not hire a spectacular venue in the UK and treat your guests to a really special weekend away with a party in a stately home, chateaux or unusual venue?

If you prefer to stay local, there's always the option of creating an incredible party in a marquee in your own back garden.

80th, 90th & 100th Birthdays

When you are celebrating one of these key milestone birthdays, you are celebrating the honorees' well-lived life. These are very personal and special occasions, and often parties where the guest of honour will be surrounded by their children, grandchildren and great-grandchildren, and watching their family grow will be one of their biggest enjoyments and achievements. Here's some really special ideas to mark a momentous occasion like this.

- Hire an impressive home where you can take all the family and make a weekend of it. Book a venue with beautiful grounds where you can throw a garden party. Lots of outdoor games for the kids to enjoy, whilst the adults enjoy a delicious afternoon tea. Choose a colour scheme to match the flowers in the gardens, add cushions and comfortable seating to add to the colour palette, beautiful tablecloths and napkins.
- Ensure your party has music that will trigger memories. It's a special way to celebrate a lifetime, bringing back favourite songs of the decades. Don't underestimate those of this age, just because it's an older generation, it doesn't mean they don't like to dance. I asked my grandma what she wanted for her 90th birthday party... she said she wanted a rave!
- Throw a This is Your Life celebration party. Get all the guests to contribute a little story to go in a souvenir book that you present to the honoree. During the event, ask

guests to tell stories, grand children to sing a special song or do a little dance, good friends and children to tell some of their favourite stories with the honoree.

- Ensure you have a photo wall/board. Bring out photos of the honoree from when they were a baby to today. Your guests will enjoy looking at all the photos from over the years.

GRADUATION PARTIES

Graduation Celebrations are all about celebrating your academic achievements. I'm not talking here about the official graduation ceremonies your university might throw, I'm talking about the celebration at home that you're going to throw with your friends and family, or you might want to throw a special party for your son or daughter. I am a strong believer that when we have worked so hard for something in life, we should be celebrating it! Here are a few graduation party ideas that you can use when celebrating at home.

A graduation party is an event that marks the end to an amazing chapter of your life. Lots of hard work has gone into getting to where you are now, so why not spoil you or a loved one with an epic grad party!

This might be a small gathering with friends and family or you may choose to have your grad pals over and have a party at home. To inspire you, below are some fun and creative ideas to throw a graduation party in style.

Create a Photo Area

To capture the best moments of your graduation party, set up a quirky photo booth. Depending on your budget, you can either hire a professional booth or create a DIY booth/backdrop. Adding signage such as "Class of (insert year!)" will create gorgeous memories you will look back on. Remember to add some fun props, graduation hats, cute signs etc. to make it extra special.

Throw a Dinner Party

We all know I love a dinner party. Theme your table to match the colours of your school/university. You can do this with coloured tablecloths, napkins and table decorations. Maybe add photos to the centrepieces of fun memories throughout your studies.

Have a Cocktail bar with a bartender

This will go down a treat and will definitely be one that's appreciated. A professional bartender on hand to make your favourite cocktails will ensure your graduation party will be one for the books. If you have underage drinkers attending, make sure you have a range of mocktails and non-alcoholic options behind the bar.

Graduation Lanterns

Ever heard of balloon release? Well, this is similar but with lanterns and creates a really special meaningful moment for those attending. Ask you guests to write wishes on the lanterns and then watch them go up into the sky.

Graduation Sweetie Station

For those with a sweet tooth, why not have a themed sweet station? Use themed witty labels to add in a special touch, such as 'Aren't you a Smartie', 'O-fish-ally Graduating', 'Teachers Pet', 'Thank you Kisses', 'Reach for the Starburst'.

Commemorative Video

A commemorative video is sure to get tears flowing. Before the grad party, get each high school guest to submit their favourite memory to you and edit these together before the big day for a touching tribute. This creates a beautiful souvenir to remember.

Create a 'Words to Live By' board.

The amount of advice that your graduation party guests can bring to the graduate is astronomical. Having a spot for guests to share their knowledge and advice for the graduate as they move forward in their life is going to be important. This can also be twinned with having motivational/inspirational quotes around the space. An alternative to this is having a words of wisdom jar.

Bright Future Bulbs

This is a really cute take home gift and one that you can easily make yourself. Give your guests light bulbs filled with sweets to take home. You can easily purchase jars shaped like light bulbs, and you can unscrew the caps and fill the bulbs with meaningful items. Attach a witty note to your gift and everyone will remember your amazing grad party. Something like, 'Here's to your Bright Future'.

Well, as you can see, I like my themed puns. Here's a few more that you can steal from me.

- Donut you forget about me (Displayed by a donut wall!)
- Shoot for the Stars (You could hire in a basketball game)
- Aloha Grad (For a tropical themed party)
- One Smart Cookie (Great to go by a themed cookie station)
- Thanks for 'Poppin' in to celebrate - (Signage to go by a popcorn station)
- She leaves a little sparkle wherever she goes (Great by a face glitter station)
- You crushed it!

New Home Parties

I love a new home party! Inviting friends and family to your home for the first time is really, really special. It's an opportunity for you to do the grand tour but also an opportunity to relax and enjoy your home and its entertaining potential. It's also about the warmth and love from your friends which a new home often lacks at the beginning.

One of my favourite new home parties of all time was in a very unique house in Alderley Edge, in Cheshire. This house was recently featured on Channel 5, in a programme called '*Sally's Posh Sleepover*', where she featured the quirkiness and extravagance of this house. The owner of this house is really into his cars, especially Ferrari's. He believes that his cars deserve a nice enough garage to match the rest of the house, so in the basement, there is an incredible garage that will fit up to 20 cars! It's no ordinary garage! It has marbled floors and floor to ceiling mirrors around the entire space, beautiful installed chandelier style lighting too. For the housewarming party we converted the garage into a party space, complete with banqueting tables and chill out furniture, a stage and a live band. It was such a special party.

Firstly, it's important to note that you don't need to rush your house warming. Enjoy your party once you are completely settled into your space, you have fully unpacked and you've started to decorate and feel excited about your space. If you find this is one to two months after you have moved in, this is totally fine. Keeping the stress levels down is more important! I always like keeping a house warming a relaxed, pop in affair. It gives you more time to spend with each of your guests. If you have the weather, enjoy a BBQ or outside affair, this way, you also keep any mess out of the house.

Celebration of Achievement

This kind of party is one you can throw at any time of year and it's one all about celebrating you. We often reward ourselves when we have done something well with a new handbag or a new piece of clothing, but why not celebrate with a party for your friends and family?

This could be a dinner party, garden party, whatever you enjoy doing most. One of my latest parties was for a public speaking and business coach, Dani Wallace, who did really well in her latest launch of her speaking programme. As a well done to herself, she celebrated her success with friends and family and it was so, so special. It was also an opportunity for her to celebrate in her dream home and invatation those who hadn't been before. Dani is full of life and character and the party had to reflect her massive personality. Dani had a tipi in her garden, with a BBQ, lots of activities for the kids, a fire pit so they could toast marshmallows in the evening, a giant swing for family photos, dressed with bright yellow and black balloons, an AstroTurf bar and lots of giant games. We themed it with a tropical twist and styled in her brand colours. It all went down a huge success and it meant so, so much to the family to be able to afford to throw a party like they did. Dani grew up on a council estate, so to get to where she is now is a massive achievement.

This is the true meaning for me of living life to the fullest and creating memories that you will remember forever. Looking back at pictures of parties like this brings so much joy.

WEDDING EVENTS

I'm super excited to share this section of the book with you. I've been planning luxury weddings for a long time. I've seen what creates an incredible celebration and I'm excited to share with you. In this section, we will be looking at all the different elements that make up the wedding celebration, pre and post wedding, and I'll be sharing with you my tips for making them extraordinary. With 100s of weddings under my belt, I have witnessed some super special moments which I will be sharing with you. All of the events in this section are wedding related.

Proposals

I love an extraordinary proposal! I'm really mushy at heart, so watching any moments like these always make me cry. It's just because these are such intimate and special moments between a couple that you can tell it's the start of two souls becoming one and the start of a life journey that's about to become really special. There are millions of ways to propose, anything from a traditional heart of red petals and candles and to proposing on a hot air balloon. A proposal needs a lot of thought going into it; think about what would be really meaningful for your partner. Do they love the outdoors? Are they an attention seeker and would love a public display? Or would they prefer something intimate and romantic? Make it special and make it personal. Proposals tend to be private, public or in a destination. I'm going to share with you some of my favourite creative marriage proposal ideas.

Private

- Plan the most romantic date night at home. Ask your partner to go out and whilst they are out, create an incredible romantic dinner set up in your own home. (If you need a little help with this, check out some of the done-for-you ideas at www.Qubeluxe.com), little shameless plug there, but they are super cute! Set the table, put on some romantic music and light lots of candles. Hire a personal chef to cook and serve a gorgeous meal and pop the ring on a plate during one of the courses!

- Create a film of experiences you have both had together over the years. You may have 100s of video clips on your phone that you have had from over the years. Edit them all together (or get someone to do it for you), mixed in with photos. At the end of the video create an extra special video, telling them you have an extra special surprise for them. As a lead up to this, hire a big screen in your back garden or somewhere really special and private, blind fold them and lead them to their own private cinema, complete with popcorn.

Public

- Propose on an airplane and use the tannoy system for the announcement
- Organise a flashmob
- Incorporate the proposal into the curtain call of his or her favourite show
- Hire a street performer and have them plan a special act, when the couple walk by, they do a scene that includes a proposal.
- Create an audio proposal, a song or podcast episode where you propose to your partner at the end. During the song/episode talk about how special your relationship is. Tell your partner you've created something special and want them to listen together.
- Plan to propose at a party. Tell the band your intentions (obviously with the permission of the host) and create a really special surprise proposal.
- Dinner with a view. My husband proposed to me in a

restaurant overlooking the old city of Jerusalem. He knew that sushi was one of my favourite foods, so he placed the ring in the middle of the sushi as it arrived!

Destination

- Take a stroll on the beach and propose in the waves of the sea.
- Propose at a romantic location such as the Eiffel Tower, Empire State Building or in front of the Trevi Fountain in Rome, Italy.
- Plan an outdoor picnic somewhere really special.
- Hot air balloon proposal.

Engagement Parties

You've had the proposal, so now comes the engagement party. This is your opportunity to share the excitement of your proposal with your friends and family. I ended up having 3 engagement parties! I grew up in Berkshire, UK, and my husband in Manchester. We had one party in Manchester for Michael's parents and friends and we had one near my parents house where my parents invatationd all their friends, and then we had a joint 'young persons' party at my parents house, which I have to say, was the most fun of all! We had a cocktail bar, we lined our driveway with pretty lights, we lit our garden up in bright colours and had a really fun evening. Here's a few unique ideas for your engagement party.

- **Wine & Cheese tasting party** - Decorate tables with beautiful florals and linen and let your guests sample brie with Beaujolais, stilton with port and gouda with Riesling, all beautiful pairings, just like you and your party. Ensure you have an experienced sommelier at your party to explain the beautiful pairings of the wine and the cheese.

- **Throw a Dessert party** - ideal with those with a sweet tooth. Include bags of popcorn with a cute message, e.g., 'He Popped the Question! Ellie & Jack are getting married!', Iced biscuits of wedding dresses, hearts and engagement rings. Incorporate strawberries, the natural heart shape of a strawberry symbolises love, pink iced donuts with soft pink roses are really pretty. Include a Donut wall that says "Donut mind if 'I Do!'".

- **Themed Afternoon Tea** - Mad Hatter's tea party style! Incorporate t-cups, floating flower heads, and use pastel colours in your linens and decorations.

- **Love Birds Cocktail Party** - Theme the party all around love birds. Drink from cocktail glasses shaped as birds. Birdcage decorations, blooming hydrangeas and birds nest style canapés.

- **Jazz inspired brunch -** A late morning soiree where guests can dig into waffles, made-to-order omelets and drink Bloody Marys whilst listening to a jazz quartet. An egg station always goes down well - have a chef and let you guests put their orders in, beautifully display all the toppings too.

- **Pool Party** - I'm imagining a floating giant engagement ring and swan inflatables in the pool, the bride-to-be dressed in beautiful white swimwear with a floaty dress. If you're not using the pool for swimming, fill the pool with giant rings filled with floating flower heads, cover the pool with balloons or floating lights.

- **Paris Party** - When you think of Paris you think of the city of Love, one of the most renowned cities in the world for romance. Throw a party with macarons and champagne, play a Parisienne playlist, artists such as Edith Piaf and Juliette Greco, twinkle lights and Eiffel tower inspired decor.

- **Shakespeare inspired party** -No one understood love better than Shakespeare, so let the playwright inspire your party. Use quotes on your invitation, use calligraphy and parchment paper to display quotes around your event space. Decorate with flowers, quills and candles and serve treats from the era. Make sure you have English Renaissance music playing in the background to create the ambience.

The Hen & Stag Parties

As we all know these can be super fun and often very wild parties! It's the last chance for the bride or groom to really let their hair down as a singleton before their big day.

The Hen party is also known as the bachelorette party in the US/Canada. The Stag party is also known as the Bachelor Party in the US/Canada and Bucks Night in Australia. When planning a stag party for someone, please consider the person involved and what they would enjoy! Taking someone really reserved out on a wild bar crawl might not go down too well, unless you know this is what they really want. Here's a few ideas to help you with your planning. You might mix and match some of these ideas for a day and night of fun. There's a little bit of something for everyone!

- Life Drawing party
- Pole Dancing or Burlesque Dance Party
- If you and your friends love dancing, you are going to love this one
- Spa weekend
- Movie night
- Farm weekend - includes cow milking, feeding animals, break making, farm trails
- Cookery classes
- Head to a festival or gig - 'Hen-Fest'
- Go to the races

- Wine tasting
- Cocktail making
- Book a karaoke booth
- Pottery making
- A relaxing yoga retreat
- Book a house in the country
- A private dining experience then a night on the town
- Bottomless brunch
- Treasure and scavenger hunts
- Murder mystery evening dinner party
- Arts & Crafts weekend - includes flower arranging, pottery and painting
- Fascinator making/flower crown making
- Glamping
- Mini Cruise
- Makeup Masterclass
- Hot tub party
- Afternoon tea or Afternoon Tease (Hosted by a naked butler)
- Body painting
- Belly dancing/Bollywood/Burlesque dancing/Can Can/Salsa dancing
- Cheerleading class with all the Pom Poms!
- Scent/perfume making
- Pamper party
- Burlesque & Cabaret show
- Explore a city on a prosecco bike
- Strip Shows
- Secret Cinema experience
- Helicopter tours with bubbles
- Chocolate making
- Comedy club
- Yoga in an unusual location
- Attend a relaxing retreat together
- Old School sports day/Olympic Shames

- White rafting
- Hovercrafting
- Go Karting
- Mud biking
- Axe Throwing
- Paintballing
- Archery
- Drone Racing
- Shooting/Clay Pigeon Shooting/Nerf wars
- Off road driving
- Escape rooms
- It's a Knockout
- Weekend breaks - explore the sights and bars of international cities.

Bridal Showers

A bridal shower tends to be a day time event celebrating the bride's upcoming marriage. The bridal shower is designed to shower the bride with good wishes and gifts. Guests usually enjoy food and drink together, play games and socialise before the big day. Usually it's the maid of honor, the bridal party or the bride or groom's mother who throws the bridal shower. These people are usually the ones to cover the costs too. A bridal shower usually lasts between two and four hours and traditionally takes place between two weeks and two months before the wedding. If you hear the term 'sprinkle', this is usually a shower for a woman who has previously been married or is having a quick wedding. It usually suggests that it's smaller than a bridal shower.

According to the history of the bridal shower, ladies in the Victorian days would gather to wish the bride well. They would bring with them small gifts, home goods and well wisher notes. These gifts were put in an open parasol and they would then 'shower' them over her.

206 · DEBBIE MARKS

Traditionally you only invatation people to the bridal shower who are invatationd to the wedding and usually all women, however this is changing and often male friends and relatives are being invatationd, so you might prefer to call it a 'wedding shower'.

I've put together some unexpected extraordinary ideas that your guest won't expect. When planning parties, if you can be creative and plan activities your guests won't expect, it will make the occasion even more memorable. Firstly, start with an unexpected location. Most people expect a bridal party to be at someone's house, but why not host it in a park (e.g., for a picnic bridal shower) or a pretty garden at a venue.

DIY Bouquets -Set up your own flower stall and have your guests choose different types of flowers and create gorgeous bouquets. These make beautiful photos once everyone has made their bouquet but also doubles up as a favour for guests to take home.

Personalised Cocktails - Ensure the cocktails reflect the bride-to-be's favourite colours/style.

Personalised Aprons & Cup Cake Decorating - Choose your favourite sweet treats such as cupcakes or biscuits and have your guests ice them. Make sure the bride has her very own 'Future Mrs' apron.

Sitting Pretty - Create a statement chair for the bride-to-be to open her presents on. This might be a chair covered with florals or with a beautiful backdrop behind it. It could be a throne or an oversized chair.

Vibrant colours & Bright coloured centrepieces - Make a statement with your decorations. Use vibrant coloured chairs and table linens and giant centrepieces, like a statement tree on a table, that will create the wow factor as guests enter.

Fun Games - Fill your bridal shower with a collection of really fun games that will have your guests in fits of laughter. Give the bride paddles that say 'I have' and 'I have not' and ask her questions. An interactive scavenger hunt is fun, that includes clues like, 'this is where the couple had their first kiss', this is where they had their first date etc.

Giant Chalk Boards - Have a chalk board and ask your guests to leave you date night ideas and marriage advice.

The Wedding

And so, the adventure begins… your planning most likely the biggest event of your life. Hopefully, you'll only be doing this once, let's help you make it magical. I have been planning weddings for the past 13 years and I can tell you, the little details really do count. Each and every special touch all counts to creating the most extraordinary wedding. If you haven't done so already, make sure you go back and follow the planning steps earlier on in this book. I'm going to share with you my top 10 tips for planning an extraordinary wedding.

1) Choose a fabulous location! - The more unusual and breathtaking your venue is, the better. This will really set the tone for the day and allow you to create something spectacular. I'm often styling events in stately homes or castles and these weddings are always so much more special than the ones in plain hotel rooms.

2) Create a Show-stopping theme - Make a statement with your decor. You can go wild and wonderful in a tasteful, elegant way. Those weddings that focus on a strong really decor theme create the wow factor. You want your guests gasping with amazement from the moment they walk through the doors due to the array of hanging florals from the ceiling, the wonderful ceremony setting, laced in florals, the abundance of candles of all shapes and sizes, or the personalised dancefloor you've had created.

3) Create a dramatic wedding aisle

The wedding ceremony is typically one of the first things guests walk into when they attend your special day, so start off how you mean to go on. Line the aisle with dramatic florals and candles, use statement arches. If you have the space, get creative with the layout of your ceremony. Could you have the ceremony in the centre of the room and guests sit all around in a circle or semi-circle? Ensure you have statement chairs and ambient lighting for a dramatic effect if taking place inside.

4) Entertainment throughout - Take care when choosing your entertainment as this is a huge part of the day that will help you create the atmosphere. Imagine a gospel choir at your ceremony, or songs from the voice of an angel as guests are entering and taking their seats. A harpist or a roaming band in your drink's reception. Book a show band for your evening reception. I've worked with some of the best show bands in the world and I can't tell you how special this is! You'll find your guests dancing the whole night, dancing on their chairs and staying right till the end of the night. The performers are truly incredible and I feel totally honoured to have been able to see so many incredible performances over the years.

5) Have fun with your food

When choosing your caterer, choose one that is happy to be creative with their food and displays it in a fabulous way.

6) Make a statement with your cake

An extraordinary wedding has to have an extraordinary cake. I once had a bride who had a nine-tier cake. She used a step ladder to reach up to the top to cut the tier. It was so special and was definitely a talking point of the day. Make sure when everyone says… 'Have you seen the cake?' they are saying it all for the right reasons. You can also display your cake in a dramatic way too. Maybe your cake is hanging on a swing, or on a beautiful mirrored table, surrounded with candles and an abundance of petals.

7) Choose a unique colour scheme

The colour scheme you choose for your wedding can have a huge impact on the look and feel of your day. Don't be afraid to be bold with your colours on your wedding day and really embrace your colour choice. Incorporate your colour scheme into all elements, including your invatations, bridesmaids' dresses, table linens and napkins, crockery and glassware and to accent pieces around your wedding. Some of my favourite statement wedding colour combinations are below.

White on white
Sage and gold
Black, white and gold
Fuchsia pink, blush and gold
Navy, blush and gold
Sage, peach and ivory
Rose gold and navy
Burgundy and blush
Forest green, gold and white
Sage, dusky blue, pale pink and ivory
Cornflower blue, greens and white
Dark teal, rust and orange
Red, purple, turquoise and gold

8) Feature Pieces

I love a feature piece and an extraordinary wedding should be full of these. This is where you create the drama. This could be thorough feature trees, floral filled ceilings, statement dancefloors, dramatic entrance ways and statement stages.

9) Layout of your tables

Be creative when it comes to the layout of your reception. Just because most venues have round tables, doesn't mean this is the layout you have to choose. Chapter 6 in this book talks about transforming your space and includes some suggestions for layouts.

10) Fabulous Florals

An extraordinary wedding wouldn't be what it is without fabulous florals. Big, bold and extravagant is definitely the order of the day. Work together with your experienced floral designer or florist to create the most incredible dramatic displays. Enormous, towering centrepieces, floral filled dancefloors, floral hanging chandeliers, flower walls, dramatic bridal bouquets and floral filled doorways and wedding ceremony decor.

Here's a checklist for planning your wedding.

12 MONTHS PRE-WEDDING

- Determine the style of wedding you want
- Book wedding planner, if you decide to have one
- Set the date
- Set your budget
- Create your Guest List
- Book your venue
- Book your registrar
- Look for Inspiration!

9 TO 11 MONTHS PRE-WEDDING

- Book a photographer or videographer
- Start shopping for your dream wedding dress
- Choose your bridal party
- Send save-the-date cards

- Book your suppliers
- Finalise the guest list
- Create or order decorations, wedding favours and centrepieces

6 MONTHS PRE-WEDDING

- Find a hair and makeup stylist and book trials
- Discuss honeymoon plans and book travel arrangements
- Shop for your bridesmaids' dresses
- Reserve accommodation, if needed

3 TO 5 PRE-WEDDING

- Order your wedding rings
- Shop for groomsmen's suits
- Meet your registrar and discuss your vows and music
- Schedule a tasting with your caterers
- Book hotel rooms for the night before/day after the wedding celebrations
- Finalise your wedding itinerary, food menu and flower arrangements
- Start to plan your hen and stag parties

3 MONTHS PRE-WEDDING

- Send out wedding invitations
- Send a shoot list to your photographer
- Have your wedding dress altered
- Start having regular facials
- Buy gifts for the best man, ushers and bridesmaids

1 TO 2 MONTHS TO GO

- Collect RSVPs and finalise the guest list for the last time

- Finish your table plan and order of service
- Book time off work
- Confirm honeymoon plans

2 TO 3 WEEKS TO GO

- Ensure bridesmaids and groomsmen have their outfits
- Give the DJ/Band any last-minute playlists
- Pack for your honeymoon
- Confirm details with all your suppliers
- Find your 'something old, something new, something borrowed, something blue

THE WEEK OF THE WEDDING

- Pack an essentials kit
- Have your hair trimmed and/or coloured
- Wear in your wedding shoes
- Order foreign currency for your honeymoon

WEDDING CHECKLIST: THE DAY BEFORE

- Have the day off to relax
- Hand over the list of supplier contacts to a designated person
- Have your nails manicured
- Eat a good dinner and try to get an early night

Wedding Anniversaries

It's so important to celebrate your wedding anniversary and yes, of course, why not do this with a party! Below you will find the traditional anniversary names and traditional gifts for each year. If you're throwing a party you might want to incorporate the anniversary name into the year.

Year	Anniversary Name	Gift or Present Idea
1st	Paper	Stationery Set, tickets to an event
2nd	Cotton	Coordinating dressing gowns, luxurious cotton sheets
3rd	Leather	Leather handbag, monogrammed wallet
4th	Fruit & Flowers (UK) Linen & Silk (UK)	Fruit basket, gardening equipment
5th	Wood	Wooden Clocks or sculptures, Wooden picture frame
6th	Sugar	Sugary treats or an afternoon tea
7th	Wool	Cozy clothing or blankets
8th	Salt	Luxury salt & pepper shakers
9th	Copper	Copper cookware, copper sculpture
10th	Tin	Candle holders, Vases, Cookware
11th	Steel	Turquoise jewellery, tulips, steel gifts
12th	Silk	Pearls, silk home decor, peonies
13th	Lace	Underwear, Silver lace, Textiles
14th	Ivory	Gold jewellery
15th	Crystal	Elegant crystal stemware, watches
20th	China	China based gifts or a trip to China!
25th	Silver	Engraved silverware, jewellery or silver tablescape
30th	Pearl	Ivory or Diamond
35th	Coral	Jade, coral inspired gifts
40th	Ruby	Ruby jewellery, ruby-red wine, red rose to plant in your garden
45th	Sapphire	Sapphire, rings, pendants, home decor
50th	Gold	Gold jewellery, cufflinks, gold trimmed glassware
55th	Emerald	Emerald jewellery, green coloured gifts
60th	Diamond	Diamond gifts
65th	Blue Sapphire	Blue Sapphire
70th	Platinum	Platinum
80th	Oak	Oak, diamonds or pearls

You will find many of the ideas in this chapter you could incorporate into a wedding anniversary celebration. My main piece of advice to you is celebrate the anniversaries, however big or small they are. Do something special with you and your partner. Even if it's just a special dinner for the two of you at home, make it memorable.

"LIFE IS
ONE BIG EVENT
IF YOU WANTED TO
CELEBRATE EVERY
DAY YOU COULD.
CHOOSE YOUR
MOMENTS AND MAKE
THEM MAGICAL."

DEBBIE MARKS

Chapter Eleven

SEASONAL & CULTURAL EVENTS

*E*very day of the year, someone is celebrating something really special. Do you have friends of different cultures who celebrate festivals that you don't understand? In this chapter, I'll be exploring with you some of the seasonal and cultural events that happen throughout the year and how they are celebrated. I strongly believe we should support each other, whatever our faith, so if we know when a friend or colleague is celebrating an important religious event or festival, the least we can do is send them a little greeting. So, from me to you, this will be your snapshot of religious festivals and celebrations - You can thank me later.

Here's an annual calendar of events to look out for and a few tips of how to make these celebrations extraordinary. Please note, the dates are a guide as to when they happen, they will vary, year on year.

JANUARY

You've packed away your Christmas decorations, the house is all clean and tidy, but now what? Where's that warmth and coziness gone? Now is the time to add warm features to your home that you can enjoy right now. January is a new year, new start and often a month of inspiration. Add feature pieces around your home that inspire you, something that lifts you up when you look at it, makes you smile and feel good about yourself.

16th Jan- Tu B'Shevat

This is a Jewish festival that celebrates the New Year for trees. It is customary for Jews all over the world to plant young trees at this time and to eat fruit produced in Israel.

25th Jan - Burns Night

For anyone of Scottish heritage, this is one of the most important and fun nights of the year, often celebrated with a Burns night supper that includes lots of Haggis, neeps (mashed turnip) and tatties (potatoes) and Whisky toasts. The day celebrates the poems and songs of Robert Burns (also known as Rabbie Burns) with a celebration meal and festivities that include poetry reading, 'Ode to a Haggis' said before the Haggis is cut, and there's lots of singing around the table. Rabbie Burns is best known for his song 'Auld Lang Syne'. A traditional starter would be Cock-a-Leekie soup and a dessert would be a Clootie Dumpling (a pudding prepared in linen cloth) or Typsy Laird (a Scottish sherry trifle). It's also typical to have some traditional Bagpipe playing or have a Cèilidh band if you were to throw a party.

26th Jan - Australia Day

Australia day marks the arrival of the first fleet of 11 British convict ships at Port Jackson, New South Wales, in 1788, and the raising of the Union Jack at Sydney Cove by its commander, Captain Arthur Phillip. It's celebrated as a public holiday. Despite its significance, it is now more of a celebration of Australia and celebrating all things great about being Australian. Outdoor concerts, community BBQ's, sports competitions and fireworks are some of the many events held in communities across Australia. This is definitely the day to throw an Aussie themed party.

FEBRUARY

1st Feb - Chinese New Year

Celebrations last for three or more days, and involve fireworks, dances (e.g., the famous Lion Dance) and gifts of paper money, flowers and sweets. Business accounts are settled and all debts paid before the New Year begins. 2022 welcomes the year of the Tiger.

6th Feb -Waitangi Day

This is New Zealand's National Day; it celebrates the signing of the Waitangi Treaty in 1840.

15th Feb - Chinese Lantern Festival

The Lantern Festival marks the first full moon of the year and the lengthening of the days. Strings of lanterns in various designs are hung up indoors and outdoors as decoration.

14th Feb - Valentines Day

Valentine's Day is **a holiday when lovers express their affection with greetings and gifts**. It is also called St. Valentine's Day. The holiday has expanded to express affection between relatives and friends.

MARCH

1st March - Christian Festival Shrove Tuesday

Relates to absolution from sin. In Britain, it's referred to as Pancake Day, as pancakes use up all the rich foods before Lent. Elsewhere it is known as Mardi Gras, and is a time for carnivals and fairs.

3rd March - Buddhist Festival Losar

This is the Tibetan New Year festival, but it is often celebrated in Nepal as well. It included a rededication of the country to

Buddhism. People celebrate by singing or dancing to traditional Sherpa songs, eating and drinking. There are many traditional ceremonial dances representing the struggle between demons and gods that are performed at local monasteries. This is the most important festival in Tibet.

17th March - Christian St Patrick's Day

Parades are held in Dublin, Ireland. A proud day for the Irish, usually celebrated with lots of drinking!

17th/18th March - Hindu festival of Holi

A spring festival lasting one to five days. Bonfires are lit and coloured powders and dyes are thrown over people.

17th March - Jewish festival of Purim

Purim is a carnival festival, recalling the saving of the Jewish community of Persia, as retold in the Book of Esther (the Megillah), which is read through twice in each synagogue. The name of Haman is drowned out with rattles and boos by the congregation when read. It's traditional to wear fancy dress, many communities have fancy dress parades for the kids, Jews have a traditional feast and it's seen as a commandment (mitzvah) to get drunk! This is a fun and lively festival. It's also a commandment to give money to charity and give gifts to the needy and to friends and family.

19th March - Muslim festival of Lailat-ul-Bara'ah (The night of forgiveness)

Muslims seek forgiveness for their sins at this time. Many hold that on this night, a person's destiny is fixed by Allah for the coming year. In many places this night is marked with firework displays.

APRIL

16th April - Jewish festival of Passover (Pesach)

An eight-day festival when Jews commemorate the Exodus from their slavery in Egypt. The Seder meal is held in each family's home at the beginning of the festival, when the story is retold in a fun way that usually gets the kids involved. The traditional greeting would be 'Good Yom Tov or Chag Sameach (Hag, Sam-ay-ah)'. Matzah (unleavened bread) is eaten throughout the festival instead of bread.

17th April - Christian festival of Easter Day

Easter Day is the most important festival of the Christian year, as it is when Christians celebrate the resurrection of Jesus. Many Easter traditions, such as the giving of chocolate Easter eggs, symbolise the gift of a new life. Many people, religious or not, use this festival to welcome Spring into their homes. Spring wreaths adorn the homes of many. Be creative with a Spring tablescape that includes Easter bunnies and spring flowers. I think it's always fun to create an experience for your kids. Why not hire an Easter bunny to stop by your house? The kids will love it!

MAY

1st May - Pagan festival of Baltaine (May Day)

Many pagans celebrate Baltaine by lighting fires and leaping over them, and/or with maypole dances symbolising the mystery of the Sacred Marriage of the goddess and god.

2nd May - Muslim festival of Eid-Ul-Fitr (Feast of Fast breaking)

This festival happens once the fast of Ramadan has been completed. It is especially a time for new clothes, good food, and presents for children. Families get together and contact friends, especially those who live far away. The community assembles for Eid prayer and a sermon at its mosques. The traditional greeting is 'Eid Mubarak', meaning a happy and blessed Eid.

5th May - Cinco De Mayo

This is a Mexican festival that commemorates a significant battle during the Franco-Mexican War. The Mexican Army, who were considered the underdogs, ended up overtaking the French and came out victorious. In the US, this is celebrated with tons of partying, food and drinks, whilst in Mexico it's celebrated with military parades and people dressed as French and Mexican soldiers. There are parades with brightly coloured floats, and they reenact the battle on its original site in Puebla. Fun fact! According to the Californian Avocado Commission, in the US, upwards of 80 million pounds of avocados are eaten on Cinco de Mayo every year. That's a lot of guacamole!

5th May - Jewish festival of Yom Ha'atzma'ut (Israeli Independence Day)

This day commemorates the declaration of independence of Israel in 1948. It is celebrated by eating Israeli foods such as falafel, shawarma and pita. Communities gather to throw parties that include Israeli dancing, listening to live Israeli music or attending concerts. Rooms are dressed with Israeli flags and all things about Israel are celebrated.

16th May - Buddhist festival Buddha Day (Vesakha Puja/Wesak)

Wesak is the biggest of Buddhist festivals. Houses are decorated with lanterns and garlands and temples are ringed with little oil lamps. People often send 'Wesak cards' to their friends.

19th May - Jewish Festival of Lag B'Omer

It recalls the end of a plague in Roman times. Weddings often take place on this day since they are not usually permitted during the rest of the Omer period. (The time between Pesach and Shavuot). This festival is celebrated by lighting a bonfire and having BBQ's.

JUNE

3rd June - Chinese Dragon Boat Festival

Great dragon boat races take place between slim rowing boats (sometimes 100 feet long) shaped like dragons. People also go down to the rivers to picnic and celebrate on boats.

4th June - Buddhist festival of Chokor

This is a Tibetan/Nepalese festival which commemorates the first teaching given by the historical Buddha. It is a colourful and relaxed summer festival. The whole community joins in processions followed by picnics.

5th/6th June - Jewish festival of Shavuot (The Feast of Weeks)

This festival celebrates the receiving of the Torah on Mount Sinai and the early harvest season in Israel. It is traditional to dress synagogues with flowers and eat dairy foods such as Cheesecake.

21st June - Pagan festival Midsummer Solstice (Litha)

This festival celebrates the Midsummer. It's a time of plenty and celebration. A traditional way to celebrate would be to build a bonfire to burn a witch. The central belief is that the fire deters evil spirits who roam freely as the sun turns south. It's a time of outdoor feasts, singing, dancing and bonfires.

JULY

4th July - Independence Day

Celebrating the birth of American independence. It's celebrated with festivities ranging from casual family gatherings to concerts, parades and barbecues. Fireworks are usually a big part of the celebrations. It's a time to wish our American friends Happy 4th July, may peace, love and happiness always be with you.

20th July - Eid al-Adha (Muslim Festival)

This is the Feast of Sacrifice and is celebrated by Muslims all over the world. It commemorated when Prophet Abraham was commanded by the almighty to sacrifice his son Ishmail. The traditional greeting is Eid-ul-Adha-Mubarak.

AUGUST

18/19 August - Hindu festival of Janmashtami/Krishna Jayanti

This celebrates the birthday of Krishna. In the temples, Krishna is welcomed with singing, dancing and sweets. The traditional greeting would be 'Happy Janmashtami'

26/27 August - Rosh Hashana (Jewish New Year)

This festival is the Jewish New Year. A ram's horn (Shofar) is blown in the synagogue, which recalls Abraham's sacrifice of a ram instead of his son Isaac. It's traditional to eat apples dipped in honey, representing a sweet new year. The traditional greeting is 'Shana Tova Umetukah'.

SEPTEMBER

The next few months are an ideal time to fill your home with some warm autumnal decorations. Prepare you home for the colder and longer nights. During this time, why not throw some autumnal themed dinner parties, really embrace the beauty of the season for its warm and vibrant tones of orange, chestnut and russet shades.

OCTOBER

10th October - Jewish Festival of Sukkot

This is a harvest festival that recalls the 40 years the Jews spent in the wilderness on the way from slavery in Egypt to freedom in the promised land. Many Jews will build a sukkah (a temporary hut) at home where they use it for eating meals and entertaining. The roof, which has to be partly open to the elements, is covered with branches and decorated with fruit. Last year, our family purchased a sukkah. Each year, we decorate it and host meals with friends.

18th October - Jewish holiday of Simchat Torah

Simchat Torah is one of the most fun days of the Jewish year. It celebrates the completion of the annual cycle of reading the entire Torah in synagogue. After seven "hakafot," rounds of parading and dancing with the Torah, the final passages of the book of Devarim, Deuteronomy are read.

24th October - Hindu/Jain/Sikh festival of Diwali

The Hindus New Year festival lasts from 1-5 days. During this time, fireworks are set off, and lights are hung out. Many dressing the entire fronts of their houses in twinkly lights. Diwali marks the beginning of the Indian financial year.

31st October - Halloween

Trick-or-Treating, costume parties, pumpkins and more. Halloween is becoming more and more of a spectacle each year, so it's time to up your game this year. Transform your home into a spook-tacular-experience, fill your front lawn with gravestones and light up your home in green. Get creative with the sweet treats, such as marshmallow and white pretzel skeletons, witches' fingers and eyeball cake pops. Throw a Hocus Pocus party. Serve glass milk bottles wrapped in bandages with stick on googly eyes to look like mummies with black straws.

NOVEMBER

5th November - British Guy Fawkes Night (Bonfire Night)

This marks the anniversary of the discovery of a plot to blow up the Houses of Parliament and kill King James I, in London, in 1605. To celebrate the night, people across Britain light bonfires, burn effigies of Fawkes and set off fireworks.

24th November Thanksgiving

This is a national holiday celebrated on various dates in the United States, Canada, Grenada, Saint Lucia and Liberia. It began as a day of giving thanks for the blessing of the harvest and of the preceding year.

DECEMBER

19th December - Jewish Festival of Chanukah (Festival of lights)

Chanukah is the Jewish festival of light. It's celebrated by lighting a menorah (9 branch candlestick). Each night, a candle is lit signifying the miracle of oil in the temple that was meant to last for 1 days but lasted for 8. To celebrate, special prayers are said each night, fried foods such as donuts and latkes (like hash browns, but better!) are eaten and parties are attended.

25th December - Christmas

Probably one of the most well known festive celebrations around the world. Celebrating Christmas in an extraordinary way has to be through super luxe decorations in the home, often designed by a Christmas design specialist. Dress your table with an opulent tablescape which adorns your table throughout December and really embrace the festivities of the season. Transforming your home to give a warm, yet cozy atmosphere with lots of special touches can make it feel so special. Fill your home with twinkly lights both inside and out.

31st December - New Year's Eve

Celebrated all over the world, a night filled with parties and celebrations and fireworks. It's an opportunity to go to town with a party at home and create a really fun evening with friends and family. I love creating themed events for New Year's. Use it as an opportunity to create the unexpected.

These celebrations are all ways that we give to our friends and family.

'Kindness in words creates confidence. Kindness in thinking creates profoundness. Kindness in giving creates love.'

— LAO TZU

"AN EXTRAORDINARY PARTY IS A FOREVER PARTY"

DEBBIE MARKS

Chapter Twelve

PLANNING WITHOUT THE STRESS

*W*ow, you made it to the final chapter. How are you feeling? Overwhelmed, excited or raring to go to plan your extraordinary party. In this chapter, I'll be sharing my top tips for planning without the stress.

1) Checklists, Checklists, Checklists

Before you start diving right into your plans, make sure you have your checklists ready to go. Make a list of everything you need to do and work your way through it, one task at a time. There are plenty of checklists in this book that you go back to and make use of. Remember, you can also download my free handy celebration planner at www.debbie-marks.com

2) Encourage teamwork

When it comes to planning, don't think you have to do everything yourself. Who around you could you delegate to, to look after certain elements of your event? Your partner might enjoy being in control of the bar or the BBQ, your kids might enjoy creating creative favours with you. I remember I roped my Grandma in when it came to planning my wedding - I had her stringing pearls onto the end of fuchsia ribbons attached to my place names.

3) Hire an Event Planner

If you are looking for a completely stress-free experience, then bring on board an experienced event planner. Do your due diligence and check their experience. The more experience they have, they will be great at troubleshooting for you, but will have the longest list of suppliers at their disposal to create a fabulous event for you. Just make sure you are really clear with your likes and dislikes and your event planner will help you pull everything together, leaving you to just relax and enjoy the process.

4) Hire an Event Designer

A truly extraordinary event requires a very talented event designer. It's always helpful to provide a designer with a mood-board of photos you like as inspiration to infuse your desires and wishes into a marvelous design.

Is an event planner different from an event designer? An event planner usually deals with absolutely everything including all the logistics, whereas an event designer focuses on the concepts and design of the look and feel of your event. There are some people, like myself, who have experience with both.

5) Hire an Event Professional to run your event on the day

You might decide that you want to plan everything yourself, you design, plan, style and coordinate, but on the day, you just want to enjoy yourself. This is where an on the day event planner comes in. They would usually meet with you in the month leading up to your event and will take the last-minute details away from you so that you can relax in the lead up to your event and not have to worry about a thing on the day.

6) Choose your suppliers wisely

Work with suppliers who you feel are confident to deliver your requirements. Look at their testimonials, how well do they know

your venue? An experienced event supplier with an excellent repu-
tation should go above and beyond to support you with any
worries you might have about your event and help you every step
of the way. You also can relax and know you don't need to worry
about them, they will just get on with it and make it happen.

7) Minimise your number of suppliers

The fewer suppliers you can work with, the less stressful it will be
as your event gets closer. Less final details meetings to have, less
people to coordinate etc.

8) Accept the unexpected

You can put as much planning in as possible, but all I ask as you
approach your event is just accept the unexpected. Things might
happen that are out of your control. If they do, you just deal with
them as they happen or just let them be and embrace it. It is what
it is and you never know, it might even enhance your event.

9) Plan with plenty of time

The earlier you start, the easier it will be. You'll have the best pick
of venues and suppliers and you can take time planning all the
little details. You might decide to get a bit crafty and make
elements yourself. Give yourself plenty of time to do some
research for your event and have fun creating moodboards to
collect your ideas.

10) Take Time to Relax

You want to be attending your big event, relaxed, chilled and in a
place of calm. Aim to have everything done the week before so
you can spend the week leading up to your event spending time on
yourself. Get all those beauty appointments booked in, a massage
and a spa day always do the trick too. When you're getting ready,
make sure you have a calming scented candle lit in the room and
play some relaxing music in the background. Remember, you are
the finishing touch to your event, so take time to really relax into

your event and just 'Be yourself & Sparkle.' - My favourite phrase of all time.

11) Get a little help…Shh it's our little secret.

I'm all about making life easy for yourself and if there is something I can do that will save me time but also make my life easier, I'll be doing it. Hire a private chef, buy ready made kits of decor (See info about Qube Luxe below), if you're not into cooking, ask your favourite restaurant to cook you up some meals and deliver to you ready to serve.

One of the things I love most about being an event planner is that I get to help people. I work with my clients at most often the most important moments of their lives and I get to experience these grand moments with them. Seeing my brides walk down the aisle or clients walk into their party to greet their guests gives me the greatest joy ever! I feel like a proud mum, just knowing they are about to truly embody the fruits of the labour they have (or we have together) put into every element of their special event.

 'There are dreamers and there are planners; the planners make their dreams come true.'

LEAVE YOUR LEGACY

An extraordinary event is a forever party. It's one that you and your friends will remember FOREVER. This is why all the little details make a difference. Make sure you are documenting every minute of your party. I highly recommend a photographer and videographer. There will be loved ones at your party that unfortunately might not be with you in years to come and the photos you can create with those people are so, so special and ones that you will treasure forever, a time where they are at their happiest with their friends and family. Throwing a party is yes, a huge investment, but you can't beat the most incredible legacy you will creating for your family.

BELIEVE IN YOURSELF & SPARKLE

This has to be my favourite phrase of all time and it's a motto that I live my life by.

"Be confident in your creations, believe that anything is possible."

"If you can dream it, you can make it happen."

"If you believe it, anything is possible."

I've always dreamt of designing events that push the boundaries by truly global standards and because of this belief, I'm now planning and designing some of the world's most extraordinary parties! - This all started with me working at home from my tiny office, with a belief that anything is possible.

Your event is an extension of you - Your best moments are yet to come.

HOW YOU CAN WORK WITH DEBBIE...

EVENT PLANNING & DESIGN FROM START TO FINISH

Debbie Marks is a multi-award-winning international luxury event designer. Debbie Marks Events brings 23 years of experience, creativity, vision and passion to your special moment, not to mention opening up her little black book of incredible entertainment and fabulous venues, to guarantee the wow factor and bring joy to any occasion. With everything taken care of, from event management to the aesthetics and the after vibe, Debbie will go above and beyond to exceed expectations for you and your guests. And that's not even the best bit, with all the hard work done for you, in a way that allows you to shine and show off your personality, you can focus on being the perfect host, and more importantly, creating magical memories with those closest to you.

THE DEBBIE MARKS EVENT PLANNING EXPERIENCE INCLUDES:

EVENT DESIGN & CONCEPT CREATION
VENUE SOURCING & SITE VISITS
SUPPLIER SOURCING FROM ENTERTAINMENT,
CATERING, MARQUEES AND MORE!
TIMELINE/RUNNING ORDER CREATION
3D VISUALS & FLOOR PLANS OF YOUR EVENT
LOGISTICS MANAGEMENT
EVENT PRODUCTION & SUPPLIER MANAGEMENT
MANAGEMENT OF YOUR EVENT BUILD, EVENT DAY
AND EVENT TAKE DOWN.

Special celebrations. Limitless potential.
Debbie would love to hear about the event you're looking to plan:
Email Debbie at debbie@debbie-marks.com

HIRE DECOR FOR YOUR EVENTS

Debbie is the founder and CEO of the Qube Decor Group, the UK's leading luxury creative and event decor company, based in Manchester. Established in 2008, Qube Events quickly became one of the most sought-after decor companies for luxury decor for Weddings, Creative Parties, Corporate Events, Christmas Decor & Bar/Batmitzvahs. The team have styled events for celebrities, society events, footballers, leading brands & venues.... Qube has its own bespoke event design studios and event decor warehouse in Manchester and works seamlessly alongside Debbie Marks Events to deliver fabulous creative events. To enquire about event decor, email info@qubeevents.co.uk. www.qubeevents.co.uk

Be inspired on instagram @qubeevents @qubeeventhire or find us on Pinterest

QUBE LUXE

Purchase Luxury Tablescapes, Event Decor Kits & Seasonal Home Decorations

 "Spoil Yourself,: you deserve it. We design it, you make it extraordinary…"

Most of us lead busy lifestyles and don't have time to spend hours sourcing the perfect combination of decor, however, we do know we want our home to look really special for the season or upcoming celebration.

Debbie has done all the hard work for you, with fabulous collections of decor for you to buy which will make you shine. Sssh, this is our little secret… created especially for you to style in your own home.

Unbox memories that last. We've taken our experience of designing large luxury live events and packaged them all up for you to bring some magic into your own home.

Available worldwide, each Qube Luxe box is created to help you show your inner sparkle and puts the magic in the memories you're creating, whatever the occasion.

Shop designs at www.qubeluxe.com

1-1 MENTORING

"To create something exceptional, an Event Professional must be relentlessly focused on the smallest detail."
When it comes to building the life of your dreams, anything is possible. We all have the opportunity in life to push forwards and I would love to help you define, and create what that means to you. So, you can showcase your personality and find your sparkle to stand out and make your mark in the events industry.

EXTRAORDINARY BUSINESS. LIMITLESS LIFE.

Whether you're at the beginning of your business journey, or have big goals to step up to the next level and attract higher paying clients, there are always challenges, but there is always a way forward. Debbie is here to help you find yours. Full of creative ideas and ambition and would love to help you achieve your business goals.

Join Debbie's free group on Facebook

'Luxury Event Business Hub'

To enquire about 1-1 mentoring opportunities email

debbie@debbie-marks.com

EVENT BUSINESS BLUEPRINT

This is Debbie's signature course, where she helps you take huge action in your business. You will learn all the key steps that you need to take to grow an event business and how to implement them. This is ideal if you're right at the beginning of your wedding or event business journey, or if you are already established and are looking to shake things up and take your business to the next level.

Find more information at www.debbie-marks.com

WHATEVER YOUR VISION, WHATEVER YOUR DREAM, WE CAN ACHIEVE IT. TOGETHER, WE CAN MAKE IT A REALITY.

How to get in touch with Debbie:

Email Debbie at debbie@debbie-marks.com

www.debbie-marks.com

Follow Debbie on Instagram @debbiesmarks

@qubeluxe @qubeevents @qubeeventhire

TESTIMONIALS

Hear what others have to say…

Debbie is one of the most creative business owners I had ever had the fortune to work with. Her mind is constantly flowing with ideas, both in the business (things to do) and for the business (things to develop). She has built a most impressive group of events-related and interlinked businesses, and her latest venture (Qube Luxe) is a beautiful demonstration of her out-of-the-box thinking, and a brilliant example of how to turn lemons into lemonade. I have no doubt that Debbie will continue to grow Qube and keep its position as a leading brand in the events-management industry.

— AMOS BEER, BUSINESS COACH & MENTOR

Debbie Marks & Qube events are a great company to use for event organisation and deliver upon the requirements of the client. Having approached a number of events businesses to support me in planning & implementing a unique private party, I found that others were not as responsive as Debbie or wanted to put forward unrealistically expensive options which would have prevented the event from taking place at all. Debbie offered a lot of creative ideas to fulfil what I was looking for whilst keeping each individual part within a reasonable price point. Her attention to detail is very good and the pace at which she responds to requests is exceptional. I would have no reservations in recommending Debbie & Qube to anyone planning a private or corporate event.

— MATT AINSCOUGH, CEO

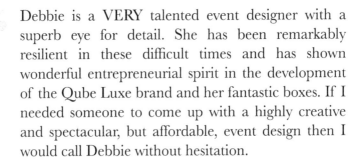

Debbie is a VERY talented event designer with a superb eye for detail. She has been remarkably resilient in these difficult times and has shown wonderful entrepreneurial spirit in the development of the Qube Luxe brand and her fantastic boxes. If I needed someone to come up with a highly creative and spectacular, but affordable, event design then I would call Debbie without hesitation.

— MIKE KERSHAW, FOUNDER OF KERSHAW
PARTNERS

We used Debbie for a whole weekend for a family Barmitzvah. Planning and organising took place 12 months before the event and every intricate detail was carefully considered and impeccably executed on the day. The result: a perfect, stress-free, enjoyable weekend. Would not hesitate (in fact would insist) on using her again.

— ROBERT GREENSTEIN

 I bought a tablescape last year from Qube Luxe and a different one this year. They are really beautiful and have absolutely everything you need for your day. I also purchased the gold partridge candle sticks which are amazing.

— NICOLE WELLS

 "Debbie and her team are amazing to work with. Their vision to create such fantastic themes blows my mind! They have endless supplies of flowers, trees, materials, furniture and props that completely transform rooms. Even though the couples/clients/organisations discuss what they are getting with Debbie, when you see the reaction on their faces to see the result is always a wow moment. Most are reduced to tears!!! I always know that a Qube Events wedding is going to look incredible. X

— CAROLINE WHITE

Lightning Source UK Ltd.
Milton Keynes UK
UKHW020633010522
402233UK00010B/347/J